BEAVERS

BEAVERS

A Wildlife Handbook

Kim Long

Johnson Books
BOULDER

Published by Johnson Books, a division of Johnson Publishing Company, 1880 South 57th Court, Boulder, Colorado 80301.
EMAIL: books@jpcolorado.com

9 8 7 6 5 4 3 2 1

Cover design: Margaret Donharl
Cover illustration: Kim Long
Photograph on page 17 used with permission of the Denver Public Library, Western History Department, Denver, Colorado.
Illustration on page 24 used with permission of the Colorado Historical Society, Denver, Colorado.

All illustrations by the author unless otherwise indicated.

Library of Congress Cataloging-in-Publication Data

Long, Kim.
    Beavers: a wildlife handbook / Kim Long.
        p. cm. — (Johnson nature series)
    Includes bibliographical references (p.).
    ISBN 1-55566-251-X (alk. paper)
    1. Beavers. I. Title.
    QL737.R632 L66 2000
    599.37—DC21   00-035234

Printed in the United States by
Johnson Printing
1880 South 57th Court
Boulder, Colorado 80301

CONTENTS

ACKNOWLEDGMENTS

Dr. Randall Lockwood, Humane Society of the U.S.
Christopher Richard, Oakland Museum of California
Gregory McNamee
Kathleen Cain
Jim Hepworth, Confluence Press
Pat Wagner and Leif Smith
The Bloomsbury Review
Denver Public Library
Western History Department, Denver Public Library
The Stephen H. Hart Library, The Colorado Historical Society
Norlin Library, University of Colorado
Auraria Library, Metropolitan State College
Bill Alther, The Denver Museum of Natural History
The Tattered Cover

INTRODUCTION

It's hard to pick a rodent with more appeal than the beaver. Cultures throughout history have found much to admire in this busy beast, often attributing to it human-based qualities such as perseverance and industriousness. Despite the fact that it exhibits these characteristics because of instinct, not learning, the beaver still manages to enthrall a wide audience.

During a long history of exploitation, it was virtually wiped out throughout most of Europe and North America. Like egrets and other birds with exotic plumage, beavers suffered from the fickle demands of the consumer market, targeted for their luxurious fur and their rich scent glands. And just as the natural beauty of birds also helped foster a movement to protect them, beavers, too, eventually benefited from their own natural appeal.

In less than one hundred years, beaver populations have grown to self-sustaining levels in most parts of their natural range and are still being actively introduced into wilderness areas where they once thrived. In some cases, the beaver success story has produced its own backlash, with the animals' instinct for gnawing down trees making them an unwelcome resident in cities and urban areas where lots of money and effort have been expended turning formerly trashed wetlands and waterways into pretty parks and green spaces.

This time around, however, beavers have achieved a new level of status. Rather than being banished or destroyed, the city landscapes that they target will be modified and protected. Unlike their ancestors, contemporary beavers will delight and inspire a new generations of humans without being targets.

THE STORY OF BEAVERS

"O my friend Ahmeek, the beaver,
Cool and pleasant is the water;
Let me dive into the water,
Let me rest there in your lodges;
Change me, too, into a beaver!"

— Henry W. Longfellow (1855, "Song of Hiawatha")

Long before modern historians began recording the impact of beavers on civilization, these aquatic creatures had an established presence. In North America, Europe, and parts of Asia, beavers were widely distributed and connected to local cultures.

Although little hard evidence exists, some experts believe that the giant beaver, an earlier relative of the modern beaver, was also part of the wildlife that humans came in contact with. In fact, the much larger giant beaver may have even provided a unique tool to these early peoples — very large and very sharp teeth that could have been used as chisels or axes.

But unhappily for the modern beaver, its thick fur, tasty meat, and oily secretion (called castoreum) made it such a valuable resource that it was hunted to extinction throughout most of its range in Europe and Asia. Once part of the native wildlife in the British Isles, it disappeared as human occupation spread, pretty much exterminated by 1300 A.D.

In 940 A.D., the earliest written record of beavers in the British Isles appeared in a set of laws published in Wales. Here, beavers and other fur-bearing animals, including ermines and martens, were declared the property of the king. Their fur was an important symbol of royal power, used in hemming the borders of garments worn by the royal family. But while wolf skins and fox skins were valued at 24 pence at that time, the beaver's skin was worth 120 pence, the most expensive in the country, and an indication that beavers were already a rare commodity.

This illustration from a book about the exploration of Canada, published in 1664, shows a typical misconception about beavers. Here, they are shown with dams constructed with human-like engineering style.

By the 1600s, only a few areas of Europe, mostly in the far northern regions of Scandinavia and Russia, had beaver populations, and by the 1800s, only a few scattered pockets of beavers remained. Still, beavers managed to make an impression on folklore in some areas of the continent, remaining a mythological image if not a living one.

A long-held belief in early European cultures was that the beaver was so frightened of being captured that it would castrate itself. To the people of the time, that was one explanation of why the beaver had no visible sexual organs. Some early Christians also associated the beaver symbolically with some saints because of this characteristic. It was thought to represent chastity in a literal sense, as in someone who kept themselves from being sexually impure. The beaver could also represent a broader philosophical concept, symbolizing a noble form of self sacrifice.

The concept of beavers castrating themselves was believed by the ancient Egyptians and supposedly written down in hieroglyphics, even though this part of the world was far from the beavers' natural range. Aristotle, Pliny, and other early Greek and Latin writers also passed along this bit of misinformation, but it began to lose credibility in the 1600s.

Also in early European cultures, the beaver was often considered somewhat mysterious because of its ability to live in the water. Because of this, some people thought of it as half animal, half fish and in the Roman Catholic faith it was once considered safe to eat

> "The ingenuity of these creatures in building their cabins, and in providing for their subsistence, is truly wonderful. When they are about to chuse themselves a habitation, they assemble in companies sometimes of two or three hundred and, after mature deliberation, fix on a place where plenty of provisions and all necessaries are to be found."
>
> — Jonathan Carver (1788, *Travels Through the Interior Parts of North America*)

beaver meat on Fridays, a day when ordinary meat was not supposed to be eaten, because it was more like a fish than an animal.

For some people, the back half of the beaver represented fish and the front half, animal. Its front feet were those of a dog and the webbed hind feet came from a swan. The beaver was also thought capable of using its tail for remarkable feats, including plastering mud and carrying building materials.

Beaver colonies in Europe were decimated or exterminated long before those in North America. When western adventurers began exploring the New World, they brought back to Europe descriptions of this animal that seemed new, not to mention strange, because for most people on that continent, beavers had already been gone for generations, if not hundreds of years. And along with the descriptions came some fanciful stories about beaver behavior.

The beavers of the New World were said to be so intelligent that they organized their colonies like human armies. Hundreds of beavers were reported to gang together in the building of cities and dams, with some beavers in charge of others.

Despite the fact that beavers had once been plentiful throughout most of Europe, by 1786, when this illustration was published in an English book, artists often ended up depicting animals that were at least a little unnatural. They relied on the observations, often flawed, of European explorers coming back from North America.

During the 1800s, beavers were gradually treated with more realism in encyclopedias and natural history reference books.

It was castoreum, however, more than meat or fur, that made beavers more valuable than other animals. Castoreum, a fluid produced by the castor glands, is a highly scented compound that beavers use to mark their territory. Beavers are able to detect the identity of other beavers, family members or strangers, from the aroma signature created by castoreum.

In ancient times, castoreum was held in high esteem by healers in many cultures; it was thought to impart special powers. One of these was as an aphrodisiac. This was not because of the scent, but because ancient cultures in Europe believed it to be a product of the beaver's sexual organs.

Because beavers spent so much time in the water, castoreum and fat from their tails were used to treat rheumatism, a human affliction often associated with damp or rainy weather.

Aside from apothecaries, who used castoreum in a variety of medicinal compounds, perfumers sought it as a base for their wares.

Beavers appear in a variety of offical symbols and the seals of several cities, including New York City and Oxford, England. Some traditional family crests from England and Canada also include the image of beavers. In heraldry, the system of designs and symbols used to denote family identity, the image of the beaver represented industry and perseverance.

The dense, oily substance was used as a base to which various fragrances were added. Perfumes made with castoreum were thought to enhance sexual energies, as castoreum was erroneously linked to the beavers' sexual activity. Even in modern times, castoreum has been used in the making of perfume, not because of any symbolic significance, but because the compound absorbs scents and releases them slowly, a valuable factor in perfume making. In the first few decades of the 1800s, at the height of the beaver fur trade, many thousand pounds of castoreum were shipped to Europe from Canada.

Popular folklore, both in Europe and North America, held that beavers provided a good indication of the severity of a coming winter. If a beaver built up a large food cache in the fall, it promised to be a long, cold winter. And if beaver fur was particularly full and thick in the fall, it was another omen of cold weather ahead.

The beaver also came to symbolize more than mythological powers, it represented wealth. In the New World, Canada in particular, fortunes were made in the beaver fur trade. In some parts of the country, beaver pelts were a form of currency and represented a standard value. Before the rush to acquire beaver fur wiped out most of the beaver colonies in North America, the wealth that beavers represented inspired the use of their image on a number of official seals, stamps, and crests.

The municipal seal of the city of New York includes a beaver, as much of the early fortune of that city came from the enterprise of John Jacob Astor (1763–1848) and other fur traders, responsible for much of New York's traffic of beaver pelts and other furs.

NATIVE AMERICAN BEAVERS

"Behold the male beaver
Of it also I, as a person, have, verily, made my body.
When the little ones make of the beaver their bodies,
They shall always live to see old age."

— Traditional Osage song

Just as with their counterparts in Europe and Asia, American Indian cultures found much to admire in beavers. With their special adaptations, beavers were a major symbol of power and force, often relating to the water. More than one tribe had origin myths that involved beavers and beavers often appeared as cunning characters in different kinds of tales.

In Alaska, myths of native cultures describe the origin of the world, when floods covered the land. In this time, Beaver Man and other legendary characters traveled around and created the animals we now know from their previous forms, which were giants and man-eating monsters.

In a Jicarilla creation myth, Cha, the Beaver, was sent by the people to stop the water from running away. He built dams, forming many lakes. The Cheyenne believed that far in the north there was a beaver that was as white as snow. He was a father to mankind and when he was angry, he would gnaw through the wooden post upon which the earth rests.

Among Sioux deities, the four traditional creative gods were Beaver, Muskrat, Kingfisher, and Flying Squirrel. White Beaver was a Seneca spirit and lived in magic water. He symbolized bad luck and disaster. The Algonquin recognized the Great Beaver, "Quahbeet," as a totem deity, but in their myths, not all beavers were major gods. And in various other myths, beaver characters did not always come out winners, or even survive.

In an Algonquin creation myth, for example, when the great flood covered the entire world, Mänäbusch, the Great Rabbit, attempted to recreate the World but first he needed a single grain of sand to start with. One by one, he sent four animals swimming

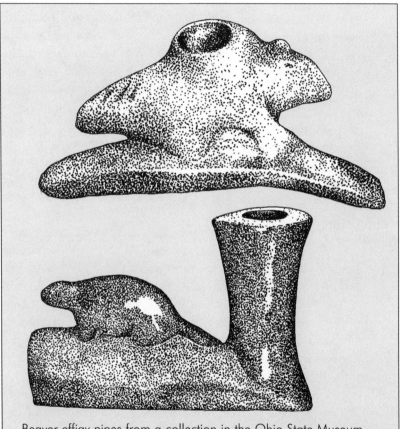

Beaver effigy pipes from a collection in the Ohio State Museum. These and other pipes were constructed by a tribe of the Hopewell culture, a pre-Columbian culture that thrived in the region of present-day Ohio from about 500 B.C. to about 500 A.D. The pipes are made of pipestone (catlinite), a soft mineralized clay found only in southwestern Minnesota and traded throughout the midwestern and eastern Native American populations.

out to find the sand and bring it back to him. The animals were Otter, Beaver, Mink, and Muskrat, but only Muskrat survived and was successful in his quest.

"Eagle and Beaver" is a Salishan myth. In this story, Eagle instructs Beaver to go and appear in front of the people, who are working at the fish weir, and then pretend to be dead. Beaver did so, and the people picked him up and carried him to their home, where they took him inside and skinned him. But then Eagle appeared and distracted the people, who ran after Eagle in order to shoot arrows at him. As all the people ran out of their home, beaver jumped up and grabbed the fire, stealing it away. He then spread the fire throughout the land.

Beaver is also involved in the spread of fire in a Nez Perce myth. According to their traditional story, before people arrived in the world, animals talked to each other just like people do. At that time, the secret of fire was known only to the Pines, and they would not share their secret with any of the animals, even in the middle of the coldest winter. But Beaver had an idea about how to uncover their secret.

The Pines got together for a meeting on an island in the Grande Ronde River (known by that name today, it is a tributary of the Snake River and flows through what are now the states of Washington and Oregon). There, they built a fire so they could get warm after swimming in the river. Beaver hid under the bank of the island and after a while, an ember from the fire rolled in his direction. He grabbed it and, holding it in his armpit, swam into the river, the Pines in pursuit. To stay ahead of them, Beaver swam from one side to the other and sometimes straight ahead. This watery path

> "Now you are lying in the water. Everything overhead that is wonderful is looking down on you, and will be pleased. Whatever you desire will be given to you. I am the oldest person, the first that Neshánu [chief] made."
>
> — Voice of Beaver from an origin myth of the Arika culture

created the meanders and straight sections of the river that exist today. Wherever the Pines got tired and gave up the chase, thick stands of pine trees now grow. Further on, scattered individual trees grow where they also gave up. Beaver swam on into the Snake River, where he shared the fire with willows, birches, cottonwoods, and others. All of these trees now have fire in them and will share it if the wood is rubbed in the right way.

In Shapatin-speaking tribes — Nez Perce and Yakima — Beaver, or Taxapul, decided he wanted all of the other diving animals to die. He decided to kill them off by challenging them to a diving contest. First, Otter accepted the challenge and went with Beaver to the water, where they dove in together in the early morning.

As the sun began to set, Otter's body floated up, lifeless, and Beaver swam to the surface the winner. One by one, the other animals failed to beat Beaver at this challenge. Then Coyote held a meeting with the remaining animals and hatched a plot to defeat Beaver. Together, Mud-hen and Mountain Woodpecker would trick him.

THE BEAVER MOON

Native American cultures often marked the passage of time with full moons, a type of lunar calendar. Tribes named these moons in different ways, typically linking them with important natural events that occurred at specific times of the year. The eleventh full moon, the one that takes place in the calendar month of November, was called the Beaver Moon by some of the Algonquin-speaking tribes of northeastern North America. This was because that was the time of year when beavers were most active and visible as they cut and stored food for the coming winter. When western colonists arrived, they borrowed the concept and the name for the same time period.

In the morning, Mud-hen and Beaver dove into the water. Unseen by Beaver, Mountain Woodpecker flew down to a canoe and pecked a hole in the bottom. Soon, Mud-hen swam up and stuck his head up through this hole, breathing the air. After a while he fell asleep and as the sun set, Beaver's dead body drifted to the surface. Mud-hen dove back down into the water and came up, the new winner.

Another tale of a contest comes from the Seneca. Turtle woke from his sleep to find his land had become covered with water. Instead of a stream, he was now in a lake with an island on it. He swam to the island and discovered Beaver emerging from it. Angrily, Turtle told Beaver he had stolen his fishing place and invaded his home. But Beaver told Turtle that if he destroyed Beaver's dam, other Beavers would only build it back again and bite his head off as well. So Turtle challenged Beaver to a contest with the winner getting to stay. The contest was to be a race and Turtle would announce the start by nipping Beaver in the tail. Turtle swam behind Beaver and bit his tail, signaling the start, but instead of letting go, he hung on. No matter how fast and far that Beaver swam, Turtle stayed right behind him. After a while, Turtle bit Beaver even harder, making Beaver so angry that he flipped his tail up over his head, launching Turtle ahead of him through the air like a flying squirrel. Turtle landed on the shore, winning the race, and Beaver had to find a new home.

A traditional Chippewa myth tells of a man who takes a woman beaver to be his wife. After a while, he began to look at his wife's sister and get hungry, thinking about eating beaver meat. He could not resist the temptation, so he killed her, cooked her, and ate her. Then he threw the bones into the water, where she came back to life. This encouraged the man, so he began to eat other beaver relatives, including his mother-in-law. Soon, other people began eating them too, but they always came back to life.

Another Chippewa story is "How the Beaver Got His Big Tail." In this myth, Muskrat originally had a tail like the beaver's and Beaver had a muskrat tail. Because the muskrat's tail was too big for its body and the beaver's tail was too small for his, Beaver suggested to Muskrat that they trade tails. So each took off his tail and swapped, then they swam together out into the lake. There, Beaver took advantage of his fine new tail and dove rapidly under the surface. Muskrat became angry when he discovered that with his new tail, he couldn't do the same. He yelled out at Beaver that he wanted to trade back but Beaver just swam away. Muskrat never got his tail again.

In a Chippewa origin myth, the hero Wenebojo envied the beavers and begged them to give him a tail like theirs, only bigger. After a lot of begging, they agreed and when he jumped in the water, he got a big tail, bigger than his own body. Happy with his new tail, he stayed with the beavers, helping them build their dam and in the winter, stayed inside their lodge. Then the Indians came and began chopping open the roof of the lodge to capture the beavers. All the beavers swam out through their tunnel, but Wenebojo forgot about his size and when he tried to follow them, he got stuck. The Indians saw his tail and pulled him out of the lodge onto the ice, where they killed him. Then they were busy catching the other beavers and killing them. The last beaver they caught was the biggest, and when they struck him, drops of blood came out of his nose. Where the blood fell, Wenebojo was brought to life again.

Among coastal tribes of the Northwest, beavers were often included as important characters in carved totems. This wooden house pole is from a traditional house built by the Haida culture, native to the area that is now British Columbia.

13

A folktale from Eskimos in Alaska tells of the adventures of Naulukkachiiyuk and his brother, who were trapped by Indians when they were coming home from a hunt one winter. Naulukkachiiyuk jumped into a beaver pond and swam until he was inside the beaver lodge, where it was clean and dry. He noticed a beaver with a strange face near the door. The father beaver told him that he could eat that beaver if he was hungry, but the beaver with the strange face, a muskrat, jumped in the water and swam away. Then the father beaver told Naulukkachiiyuk that he could eat one of his children. Naulukkachiiyuk did this, but the rest of the beavers left. Not wanting to go outside, Naulukkachiiyuk remained in the beaver house for a long time and got hungry again. There was nothing left to eat, so he began eating parts of his clothes, including his parka.

After a while, he got skinny and made a hole in the roof of the beaver house. Sticking his head out of the hole, he discovered that it was now spring. He went outside and found his brother, who had died. After burying him, he went home and gradually ate enough to

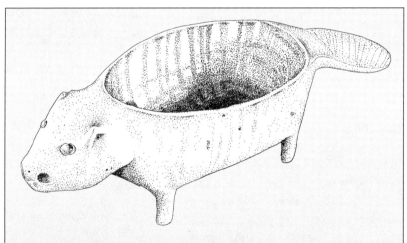

This carved effigy bowl in the form of a beaver dates to the last half of the 1700s. It comes from the Kaskaskia culture that was native to the region that is now Illinois and Indiana.

gain back his lost weight. Then he went looking for the Indians who had trapped him. When he discovered their village, he waited until they had all gone into their house, then blocked the door with logs and used fat and willows to burn the house down.

The Algonquin myth about the origin of the beaver relates how a family was crossing a river when the mother and children were swept away by the rushing water. Later, the mourning father returned to the spot and discovered they had been transformed into beavers. Calling to him, he was drawn into the river where he, too, was turned into a beaver.

In the Haida culture, Porcupine stole Beaver's food cache, but refused to admit it. Beaver and Porcupine began to fight and Porcupine stuck Beaver with his sharp quills. Then Beaver's father gathered together all of the Beaver people and they attacked Porcupine's house, capturing him. They took him to an island in a river, where he was left by himself. Calling for help, Porcupine found that no one could hear him, so he sang a magic song to summon the North Wind, which caused the water in the river to freeze.

When the ice was solid, Porcupine's father and friends crossed over and rescued him from the island. Then, all of the Porcupine people gathered together and attacked the Beaver people. Beaver was taken captive and the Porcupines carried him to the top of a tall tree, where he was left alone. Since Beaver could not climb, he used his teeth to cut off the tree, piece by piece from the top down. Then he disappeared. After that, there was no more war between the Porcupine people and the Beaver people.

In a Blackfoot origin myth, the young hero Apikunni sets out on an adventure. During his journey he lay down next to a beaver's lodge, fell asleep, and began dreaming. In his dream, an old white-haired beaver invited him to come into his lodge. There, Apikunni stayed through the entire winter and from the old beaver learned songs and secrets of healing. In the spring, Apikunni left the lodge, and old beaver gave him a special bag of medicine, a tobacco seed, and a long stick from an Aspen tree.

Apikunni and his friends, who had waited for him, set out for home but were followed by one of their enemies. Using his new powers, Apikunni dove into the water and swam behind the enemy, then killed him with the Aspen stick. This was the first person to be killed in battle. Then Apikunni returned home, introducing tobacco to the people.

The Kwakiutl culture of the northwest related the myth "Beaver Makes a Flood." The women of a village were digging clover roots next to a river and across from them on the other side were a group of young men who called to the women, wishing to visit with them. Marten called and the women liked how he looked, so they sent a canoe over to pick him up. Raccoon called and the women liked his striped face, so they sent for him. Then Snake called and they accepted him, followed by Stone-Worker-with-the-Feet, Otter, who was also picked up.

Finally, Beaver made his call and the women asked "What Beaver are you?" Beaver replied, "I am Tree-Feller," and the women asked "Who are you, Tree-Feller?" An angry Beaver shouted "I am Dam-Builder," and the women asked "Who are you, Dam-Builder?" Beaver answered, "I am Swimmer-Downstream-on-the-Belly." "Who are you, Swimmer-Downstream-on-the-Belly?" After all this, the women still made fun of Beaver, suggesting he should stay where he was, where his stomach would grow fat. Beaver went into the water and called to the sky, making it rain. But the women didn't care, having blankets for cover, so Beaver called for more rain and soon the river rose and washed the women away into the bay, where they turned into frogs.

In the Seneca creation myth, Sky Woman is banished into a great hole where there is nothing but water. She survives when the animals gather mud and place it on the back of the turtle, forming land. Then she made the sun and moon and turned groups of stars into constellations. The constellation that we call the Little Dipper became Nan-ga-ni-a-gon Ga-sa-do, or Beaver that Spreads its Skin. It follows people whenever they travel at night, always pointing to the North Star.

Among the Wishom there is the story of Is-tam-ma, the Chief of

Among the Osage Indians, beavers were used to make hats that were part of this culture's traditional costume. This photograph was taken in an unknown studio in the Oklahoma Territory sometime in the late 1800s or early 1900s. From the photography collection of the Denver Public Library, Western History Collection. Used with permission.

the beavers. A boy and his sister lived near a lake that was full of beavers. The girl had an unusual head of hair, dry and stiff, and the boy tried hard to kill birds and other animals in order to get oil for her to use on her head. Nothing worked, so the boy made a bone spear and killed one of the beavers in the lake in order to obtain oil from the fat in its tail. First he killed one, then another, and finally almost all of the beavers, collecting their tail oil.

Still, he wanted more oil, so he went after the very last beaver, a small animal that would not provide much oil, but as it was the only one left, he must have it. He threw the spear and struck the tiny animal and it immediately began to grow, becoming very large. The mighty beaver then pulled the boy into the lake because he would not let go of his spear.

This beaver turned out to be from the ocean and he was known as Is-tam-ma, the greatest beaver of all. Is-tam-ma pulled the boy across the water and broke through the mountains, draining the lake, then sped down to the ocean. Along the way, the boy grabbed onto the branches of pine trees and the roots of willow trees, trying to save himself, but Is-tam-ma continued to pull him along. Then the Grandfather bulrush called out to hold onto him, and the boy did, stopping Is-tam-ma, who pulled and pulled, but couldn't make the bulrush break loose.

> "You talk about and fear me;
>   You talk about and fear me.
> As like the sinuous snake
>   I go upon the water.
> I see that you go slowly;
>   I see that you go slowly.
> Strong as the Sun among the
>   trees,
>   You leave your mark upon
>   them.
> Younger brother, I am Beaver,
>   I am the quick-eared Beaver
> That gnaws the trees of the forest,
>   'Tis I who overthrow them."
>
> "Beaver Song"
> — traditional song of the Pima

Finally, Is-tam-ma rolled over in the water, dead. The boy cut the giant beaver into pieces. He threw several pieces onto the nearby land and they became the tribes. He saved only the tail, which he took home and cooked to make oil for his sister's hair. With this oil, she turned into the gills of the salmon.

In a tale of Coyote and Beaver from the Klamath culture, Coyote tricked Beaver's three sons into laying down on hot rocks so they would be cooked, making a meal for him. Later, he denied he had eaten them, but Beaver did not believe what he said and tried to attack him. So Coyote ran away, expecting his speed to keep him out of danger. But everywhere he ran, he looked back and saw Beaver following. When they came to a lake, Beaver created a rushing river, trapping Coyote. Then he held Coyote under the water until he drowned, making him a Coyote forever.

The Kutenai have a myth regarding the deluge. Yawóonik, the Deep Water Dweller, or monster, swallowed Duck, the brother of Red-Headed Woodpecker. To keep the monster from getting away by swimming up a stream, Woodpecker sent Beaver to build a dam. The monster was trapped and Woodpecker slit open his stomach, releasing his brother.

BEAVER MEDICINE

"There is in the composition of every man, whatever may be his pride in his philosophy, a proneness in a greater or less degree to superstition, or at least credulity."

— Rev. John Bachman (1851, *The Quadrapeds of North America*)

Beavers earned a long-lasting reputation for their contribution to the healing arts, thanks to their smelly secretions. Castoreum, secreted from two castor glands found near the base of the tail, is used by beavers to scent-mark their territory, a practical and vital part of their survival amid competition from other beavers. The yellow-to-orange colored liquid is normally spread on piles of dirt or other debris along the banks of a beaver's territory. The castor glands of four to six adult beavers is required to produce about a pound of castoreum.

This secretion has long had an attraction for humans as well. In both European and North American native cultures, the compound developed a reputation for its ability to heal a variety of ailments. These include headaches, deafness, abscesses, gout, epilepsy, colic, toothache, sciatica, lethargy, fever, pleurisy, tuberculosis, arthritis, and rheumatism. It was also thought to induce sleep as well as prevent sleepiness, and in some cultures, women believed it would induce abortions. Kwakiutl Indians made a laxative from castoreum. The compound was dried and stored and when needed, mixed with water.

Hippocrates, the noted Greek considered to be the father of medicine, was among many authoritative figures who recommended castoreum for its curative powers. In the Middle Ages in Europe, applications for castoreum included its use as a tonic for the bites of snakes and spiders, a preventative for deafness, an aid to improving memory, an antidote for bad eyesight, and a cure for "dropsy" (a swelling or tumor) or just for the reduction of tumors. Not only that, it was reported to cure hiccoughs and had the reputation of repelling fleas. Some people believed that when sniffed, it could induce sneezing.

Medical folklore has also imparted special meaning to beaver teeth, a prominent part of its anatomy that helped make the animal a champion among gnawers. People wore beaver teeth as amulets around the neck, believing this would restore strength and vitality to failing human teeth. For children, beaver teeth could be strung around their necks as a potent talisman when they were teething. A Cherokee superstition involved the loss of baby teeth by children in the tribe. When one of these teeth dropped out, the child was sup-posed to run around the house, repeating "Beaver, put a new tooth into my jaw" four times. Then the tooth was thrown upon the roof.

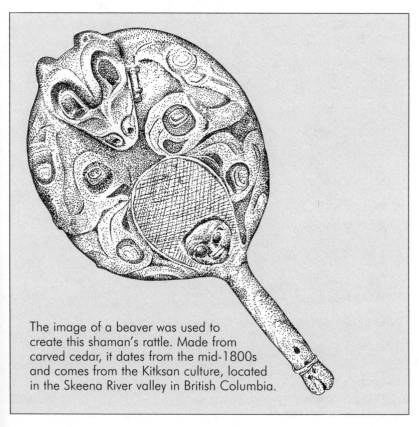

The image of a beaver was used to create this shaman's rattle. Made from carved cedar, it dates from the mid-1800s and comes from the Kitksan culture, located in the Skeena River valley in British Columbia.

BEAVER SPOTS

In the United States, "beaver" appears as a name on many natural landscape features. Geographical locations in the United States named for the beaver number almost 3,500. One of the most prominent is "Beaverhead Rock," a natural rock formation in the shape of the head of a swimming beaver. Located in southwestern Montana, this site was recognized and used as a reference point when Sacajewea guided the Lewis and Clark Expedition through the area in 1805. Among the natural geographic features in the United States that include the word "beaver" are ...

- 3 bars
- 9 basins
- 16 bays
- 1 bench
- 1 bend
- 12 capes
- 8 cliffs
- 12 falls
- 48 flats
- 2 forests
- 13 gaps
- 23 islands
- 331 lakes
- 7 mountain ranges
- 53 parks
- 2 rapids
- 29 ridges
- 1 slope
- 38 springs
- 73 summits
- 61 swamps
- 55 valleys
- And 1,373 creeks and streams

In addition, 197 man-made sites feature the name, along with 26 post offices, 27 trails, 2 tunnels, 2 wells, 141 dams, and 154 towns, cities, and sub-divisions.

Beaver fat, obtained from the tail or carcass, was also used as a medicinal compound. It was recommended for treating epilepsy, muscle spasms, asthma, dysentery, light-headedness, toothaches, and convulsions. As a preventative, it could also be used to ward off lethargy and apoplexy (stroke).

Some North American Indians were also reported to use the compound in conjunction with tobacco, creating a soothing effect. They valued it to prevent frost bite or to treat it and it was used as a salve to treat rheumatism. Beaver skin shared some of these properties; it was a treatment for colic (spasms of the colon), muscle spasms, consumption (tuberculosis), and bed sores.

Castoreum has now been found to contain salicyclic acid, possibly produced from the bark of willow trees, part of the diet of beavers in many locations. Salicyclic acid is the main active ingredient in aspirin. But despite this chemical presence, the use of beaver-based compounds for healing have faded away and there are currently no mainstream medical applications.

Some American Indian tribes held the beaver in special esteem because of its apparent powers. For those Indians who hunted beavers for food or fur, the animals were treated with respect so as not to anger their spirits. Hunters in some tribes would not let their dogs eat beaver bones, for example, as this might make the beaver spirits prevent them from catching more beavers. Among the Tlingits, if the meat of the beaver was fed to dogs, the spirit of the dead beaver would tell the spirits of living beavers that this had happened.

Among the Salish tribes, beaver skulls were sometimes placed on the top of poles or stuck in trees. It was believed that beavers, along with bears, had the ability to see and hear everything, including whether anyone was hunting for them. Thus, if a hunter killed a beaver, it was only because the beaver knew it and allowed it out of pity. By placing a beaver skull as a totem, the beaver's spirit might be more likely to appreciate the hunter's good will.

Some Native American tribes in the midwest thought that the spirits of humans were trapped inside beavers and that by killing the

Beavers were sometimes used by Native American tribes to make bags for tobacco or medicine. This traditional Sioux tobacco bag was made from the whole skin of a beaver and was used as a tobacco pouch. The pouch is decorated with porcupine quill embroidery and was carried with the head hanging from the waist, suspended from a belt or sash. The bag was used to carry tobacco (probably kinnikinic, a native plant that was sometimes referred to as "Indian tobacco"), a tobacco pipe, and the equipment needed to start a fire, usually flint, fire-stell, and touchwood.

This illustration, from a picture titled "Indian Pouches for K'nich-K'neck," is by George Catlin (1796–1873), from *The Manners, Customs, and Condition of the North American Indians*, written and published by Catlin in 1841. Reproduced with permission from the collection of the Colorado Historical Society, Denver, Colorado.

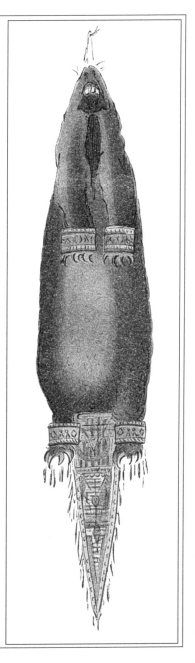

BEAVER IS THE WORD

The English word beaver came from a Scandinavian root, probably introduced into the language by Norse invaders in England. In Old English, the word was "beofor." At different times it was also spelled "befor," "byfor," "befer," and "bever." The root word probably came from "bebru," an Old Teutonic word that simply meant brown or brown animal. In Old Aryan, a similar form was "bhebhrú," which meant brown water animal and before that, it may have been the Sanskrit word "babhrús," also meaning brown or large mongoose.

The scientific name, "castor," is the word for beaver in Latin, and in Greek, it's "kastor." The root of this word may have been borrowed by the Greeks from Sanskrit, where the word "kasturi" meant musk. The Latin form "castor" was used as the formal scientific name of the beaver species and the genus name for the European beaver is "fiber," one of the original Latin words designating this animal. The genus of beavers in North America is "canadensis," a word signifying the Canadian territory.

"Beaver" has had a long history as a word used to designate things other than the animal it now refers to. In the Middle Ages in England — spelled either as "bever" or "bevor" — the word meant a between-meal drink or snack, a use that led to the modern word "beverage." As a verb, "bever" meant to tremble, to shiver, or to quake. Spelled either as "beaver" or "bever," it could also refer to the movable visor or face-guard used on military helmets. In some parts of the British Isles, "beaver" or "beever" referred to brambles or undergrowth growing next to hedges. The person's name "Beverly" originated with St. Beverly, or St. John of Beverly, a pious priest who founded a monastery in a town in Yorkshire, England, around 700 A.D. Beverly got his name because beavers were once common in that area; it's a combination of "beofor," the Old English word for beaver and "leac," meaning stream.

THE LANGUAGE OF BEAVERS

ALBANIAN bebras

ANGLO-SAXON béofor

BRETON bieuzr

BULGARIAN bobyr

CATALAN castor

CHINESE hélí

CORNISH befer

CROATIAN dabar

CZECH bobr

DANISH bæver

DUTCH bever

ESPERANTO kastoro

ESTONIAN kobras, piiber

FAROESE bævur

FINNISH majava

FRENCH castor

GAELIC dobhar-chu

GAULISH bibrax

GERMAN biber

GREEK kastôr

HAWAIIAN piwa

HEBREW boneh

HUNGARIAN hód

ICELANDIC bjór

INDONESIAN berang-berang

IRISH béabhar

ITALIAN castoro, castorino

JAPANESE biba, kaira

LATIN fiber, castor

LATVIAN bebrs

LITHUANIAN vebras, bebras

LUXEMBOURGISH biber

MALTESE kastor

NORWEGIAN bever

PERSIAN sagiábí

POLISH bóbr

PORTUGUESE castor

PUNJABI uddh

ROMANIAN castor

RUSSIAN bober

SERBO-CROATIAN dabar

SLOVAK bobor

SLOVENE bober

SPANISH castor

SWEDISH bäver

TURKISH kunduzu

UKRANIAN бообер

WELSH afanc

AMERICAN SIGN LANGUAGE

The sign for "beaver" is made by holding both hands out in front of the chest. With the right hand held over the left hand, palm down, move the right hand up and down several times, slapping the palm of the left hand.

beavers, these spirits were free to become humans again. For this and other reasons, not all Indians hunted and ate beavers. One clan of the Cheyenne, for instance, believed that the father of mankind was a great white beaver. If he became angry, he would gnaw through the wooden post that held up the earth. If these clan members touched the skin of a beaver or ate beaver meat, they believed they would become ill.

Among the Lakota, the Beaver spirit is named Capa and is the patron of work, food provisions, and faithfulness. In some subarctic tribes, this animal is known as Dunne-Az, or Beaver Doctor, and has special healing powers. People who are sick can be healed if they have dreams about being inside a beaver lodge.

In the Fox tribe, some members belonged to the White Badges, an association with a special wand decorated with beaver fur, sweet-grass, and crow's feathers. A Chippewa hunter would use the pelvis of a beaver, held in the left hand, while making a prayer for a successful hunt. The Chippewa also used bits of beaver tail and tail fat as fishing charms.

Among the Blackfoot, beaver bundles were used for certain rituals, including the tobacco ceremony. Such a bundle was made from a large beaver skin and other animal skins, held together with stitches meant to represent the marks of the beaver's teeth. The bundle contained a packet of cattail stems as a symbolic food offering for the beaver, along with tobacco seeds.

Pawnee medicine men kept albino beaver skins as a talisman. To the Pawnee, Kitkehahki was the keeper of the Beaver medicine. All the power of this medicine originated with an albino beaver and the skin of albino beavers was thought to hold special powers.

The Comanche, too, believed that the beaver was responsible for special healing powers. Their "Big Tail Medicine" ceremony originated when a man who was fasting in the mountains had a vision in which Beaver taught him to perform healing rituals for those that were sick. In this ceremony, a large tipi was put up by combining the poles and coverings from two ordinary tipis.

On the east end of the tipi, a deep ditch was dug to represent the

AMERICAN INDIAN LANGUAGES

Just as with other important animals and parts of their environment, some native American cultures, especially those in the far north, used more than one term when referring to beavers. Different words were used for baby beavers, young beavers, two-year-old beavers, adult beavers, male and female beavers, family groups, etc. The words in this list represent only the most generic terms.

ABENAKI   amisk, dademakwak
ALABAMA   ofàta ayeksa
APACHE   chaa, cha
APSAROKE   bidúpe
ARAPAHO   ho'miïhomi'ï
ARIKARA   chítu
ASSINIBOIN   chápa
BILOXI   tama
BLACKFOOT   ksiskstaki
CAHTO   chin-tii'aalh
CAYUGA   naganyá'gǫ'
CHEROKEE   do'ya
CHEYENNE   hómae
CHICKSAW   foci
CHINOOK   eena
CHIPPEWA   ah-mik
CHOCTAW   kinta
COCHITI   kúu
COMANCHE   pámouetz
COWLITZ   ƛláktlk
CREE   amisk
CREEK   Itchàswàlgi
DELAWARE   amóchk

FLATHEAD   skaléu
GROS VENTRE   ábesia
HAIDA   chun
HIDATSA   midhúpu
HOPI   pahona
HUPA   ca
INUIT   kiggiark, pahlook'ta
INUPIAT   paloKtoK
IRIQUOIS   nagaia''gi'
ISLETA   pachaídé
JEMEZ   wázi^n
KIOWA   pou
KWAKIUTL   kol, kólon, tsôw
LAGUNA   kóo
LUMMI   skáiau
MAKAH   kató
MANDAN   mádhap, warrahpa
MENOMINEE   nomäí
MIAMI   amehkwa
MICMAC   kopit
MINGO   unökanya'kö
MUSKOKEE   echaswv
NARRAGANSETT   nóosup

NATCHEZ Emet ōwàts

NATICK t'makwa, tummûnk

NAVAJO chaa'

NEZ PERCE táx̣cpol

NOOTKA átú, kató

OJIBWAY mik

ONONDAGA nagarriáki

OSAGE zhá-be

PAPAGO kâvi

PENNACOOK tmakwa

PEQUOT tûmúnk

PIMA kohwih, kokowih, kâvi

POMO tihnár, kátkea

POTAWATOMI muk

SHAPITAN wishpúsh

SALISH tsáwi

SAN ILDEFONSO tyugí

SEMINOLE etshasswah

SHAWNEE amaghqua

SIOUX chápah, champah

SNOHOMISH ṣṭukh̃u

SPOKANE skul-le'u

TANAINA chu

TAOS pâyána

TEWA óyo, ojo

TUSCARORA jonockuh

UTE powinch

WAPPO menaáwi

WIYOT hiyuwúlik

YUPIK paluqtaq

YUROK téghá

ZUNI píha

SIGN LANGUAGE

Among some North American tribes, the word for beaver could be "spoken" with the hands in a universal sign language understood across many cultures. To make the sign for beaver:

"Hold extended left hand, back up, pointing to right and front, in front of body, left forearm horizontal; bring the extended right hand, back up, under and at right angles with the left, back of right resting against palm of left hand; lower the right hand by wrist action, and raise it, back of right striking against left palm sharply; repeat motion."

From *The Indian Sign Language*, by W.P. Clark, published in 1885 by L.R. Hamersly & Company.

underground entrance to a beaver lodge. In the center of the tipi was a pool of water, and willow branches and a small willow tree were stuck in the ground on the west end. An earth mound on the side represented the lodge and another mound was constructed in the shape of a beaver. On this symbolic mound, the patient would lay down while rituals were conducted. The rites included singing, prayers, body manipulation, and the use of a "bull roarer," a traditional noise maker. This ceremony continued on and off for up to two days and nights.

Beavers were not only used for religious symbolism, they also provided practical items that were used by many tribes. Other than the obvious value of the thick fur, the castor oil was sometimes used as a hair dressing and perfume. The Apsaroke also made a glue by boiling the membrane obtained from beaver tails and the scrapings from hides. This glue was used to fasten bowstrings to bows.

BEAVER MYTHS

"There cannot be a greater imposition, or indeed a grosser insult, on common understanding, than the wish to make us believe the stories of some of the works ascribed to the beaver ..."

— Samuel Hearne (*A Journey from Prince of Wale's Fort in Hudson's Bay to the Northern Ocean in the years 1769, 1770, 1771, and 1772*)

Beavers are one of the most fascinating of all animals, with many unique characteristics and activities. Despite their impressive natural talents, however, people have a long history of endowing them with extra mythical capabilities. Beaver tails were thought to be one of their most important tools, used to pound sticks into the mud and carry material to dam sites. And as busy as they are, beavers were once believed to work all the time, never sleeping. Living in a watery environment, many people long believed that beavers ate fish.

For centuries in Europe, it was believed that male beavers had no visible sexual organs because they would bite them off when cornered. Further, some people thought that beavers being chased would suddenly stop and rise on their hind legs, facing their pursuers to indicate that they were missing these organs. Supposedly that would end the hunt, as the castor glands were often target of beaver hunters in Europe, and in ancient times, these glands were confused with the testicles.

Folk wisdom held that beavers could predict the weather, with extra large caches of food in the fall or extra long fur meaning a long, hard winter on the way. Puzzled by the ability of beavers to stash branches at the bottom of their ponds, some observers believed they would suck the air out of the wood in order to make it sink.

As superior "axmen," beavers were thought to be able to cut trees

In this illustration from a book published in 1738, a beaver colony is depicted with several exaggerated and fanciful characteristics, including a group of beavers coordinating their efforts to fell a tree.

so as to make them fall toward the water. They were also credited with cutting partway through a tree trunk and letting the wind blow trees over. As superior engineers, they were thought to fell trees so they would make natural dams. And sensitive to the level of water stored behind their dams, some thought that beavers slept in their lodges with their tails in the water so as to detect any sudden change in depth.

BEAVER
VITAL STATISTICS

NORTH AMERICAN BEAVER
Castor canadensis

VITAL STATISTICS

NAME	**Beaver** *Castor canadensis* **FRENCH/SPANISH** castor/castor		
DESCRIPTION	Largest rodent in North America. Stout rounded body with rounded head and large, flat, paddle-shaped tail; small rounded ears; prominent front incisors. Body and front part of tail thickly furred. Color brown, dark brown, reddish brown, yellowish brown or black with lighter underparts; feet and tail very dark to black. Five claws on each foot; rear feet webbed. No size or coloration difference in sexes.		
COMPARISON	Sometimes confused with a muskrat or nutria. The beaver is much larger than a muskrat, which has a long rounded tail. The nutria is about the same size as a beaver but has a long rounded tail.		
TOTAL LENGTH	24–40 inches 60–102 cm	TAIL LENGTH	10–18 inches 25–45 cm
WEIGHT	24–60 pounds 12–27 kg	TAIL WIDTH	4–5 inches 10–13 cm
TEETH	20 teeth [Incisors 1/1; cuspids 0/0; premolars 1/1; molars 3/3]		
HABITAT	Always found in or near water, including streams, rivers, and lakes. Elevations from sea level up to about 10,000 feet (3,050 m). Prefers areas with access to aspen, poplar, willow, or birch. Colony territories range from 10–75 acres.		
LODGING	Throughout most of its North American range uses lodges constructed of branches, twigs, and mud in lakes or streams. Lodgings may be completely surrounded by water or partially on land. In some streams and rivers, lodgings may be burrows dug into banks, with underwater entrances.		

35

RANGE

Approximate normal
range of species.

FOOD	Herbivore. Primary diet of inner bark, twigs, leaves, and shoots of trees, especially poplar, aspen, willow, and cottonwood, as well as alder, birch, beech, maple, and oak. Also eats grasses, water plants, algae, moss, water lilies, fruit, and berries.
PREDATORS	Young beavers are preyed upon by wolves, coyotes, dogs, owls, hawks, fishers, martins, wolverines, otters, fox, lynx, and bobcat. Adult beavers may be taken by bears, wolves, coyotes, and dogs.
BREEDING	Mating occurs from January to March; gestation period of about 120 days. Litters range from two to six in number; newborn kits weigh 8–24 ounces (225–680 grams) and are born with fur and with eyes open; weaning at six months. Adults are usually monogamous and often mate for life; young beavers usually begin mating when they are two to three years old.
VOCAL CALL	Distinctive alarm call made by slapping the tail against the surface of the water. Calls include hoarse chatter and low musical "whining" tone.
HABITS	Usually most active in early mornings and evenings; mostly nocturnal in their current range. Often lives in extended families with more than one generation in the same lodge. Migrates to find new sources of food and safe water conditions. Does not hibernate but is relatively inactive during extremely cold weather, living off of underwater caches of food.

BEAVER SIZE COMPARISON

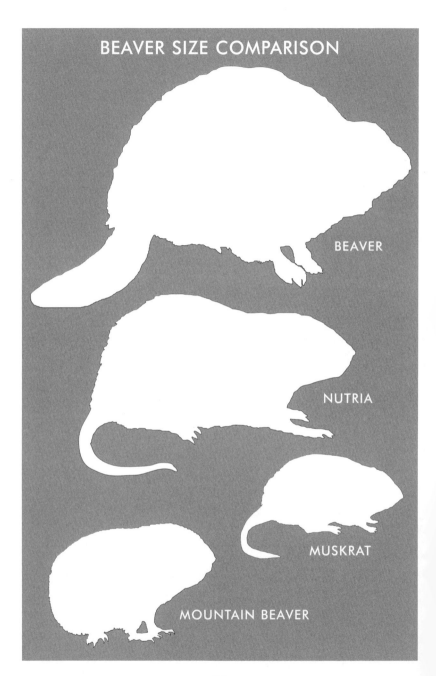

BEAVER

NUTRIA

MUSKRAT

MOUNTAIN BEAVER

THE UNBEAVER

The beaver that is not a beaver is the mountain beaver. Also called the sewellel, this rodent belongs to a taxonomic family that is separate from that of the beavers profiled in this book. Mountain beavers (*Aplodontia rufa*) inhabit a limited range in North America, extending from southern British Columbia southward through northern California. Almost tailless, this animal is small, from 12 to 18 inches in length (200–460 mm), and despite its name, lives neither in the mountains or in the water. Mountain beavers are found from sea level up to about 7,000 feet in elevation (2,135 m) and live in burrows dug in the soil. They eat a wide variety of plants, including the bark, leaves, and small branches of trees, possibly inspiring its name. Compared to all other rodents, scientists believe that this animal is the most primitive.

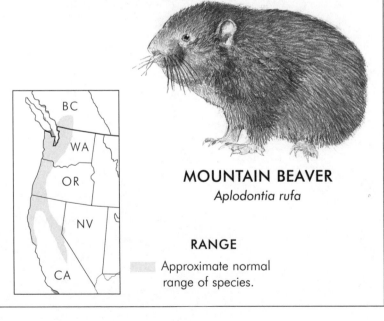

MOUNTAIN BEAVER
Aplodontia rufa

RANGE
Approximate normal range of species.

THE NUTRIA

The nutria is sometimes confused with the beaver. Although these animals are both rodents, only the beaver is native to North America. Beavers are not only larger than nutria, their tails are distinctly different. Beaver tails are flat and wide, shaped like a paddle. Nutria tails are long, thin, and round, similar to the muskrat. Nutria do not build lodges, but use burrows dug into the sides of streams or lakes.

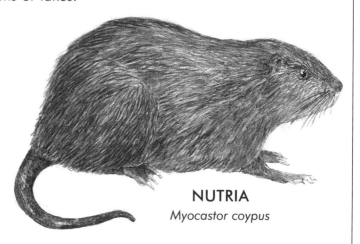

NUTRIA
Myocastor coypus

RANGE
Approximate normal range of species.

THE MUSKRAT

Muskrats share almost the same range in North America as beavers and live in the same kind of watery environments. Muskrats are sometimes confused for beavers, but they are much smaller and do not have the broad, flat tail that is characteristic of beavers. Muskrat tails are fully furred and are long and thin.

MUSKRAT
Ondatra zibethica

RANGE

Approximate normal range of species.

EVOLUTION

"Would I to enumerate every instance of sagacity that is to be discovered in these animals, they would fill a volume and prove not only entertaining but instructive."

— Jonathan Carver (1788, *Travels Through the Interior Parts of North America*)

Most taxonomists believe that there are only two species of beavers in the world. In North America, there is *Castor canadensis*, the North American beaver, and in Eurasia, *Castor fiber*, the European beaver. Previous taxonomic arrangements made a place for more species, in some cases dozens. This understanding was based on the variety of sizes and colorations that characterize beavers, as well as extremes of habitat where they were originally observed.

In North America, some authorities list subspecies for this continent's beaver population. Subspecies include the Canadian beaver, the Michigan beaver, the Newfoundland beaver, the Rio Grande beaver, the Missouri River beaver, and the golden-bellied beaver, among others. In Europe, subspecies may include the Scandinavian beaver, the Rhone beaver, the Elbe beaver, the Polish beaver, the Ural beaver, and the Mongolian beaver.

Even if subspecies are a provable distinction for beaver populations, migration and interbreeding make it difficult to keep them separate. Particularly in the 1900s, beavers from local native populations were live-trapped and shipped to areas where populations had been long gone. Thus, even if a particular subspecies had been native to one area, by now it may have been replaced by another through human effort.

In general, whether due to subspecies characteristics or general adaptations to climate, beavers in the northern parts of the North American range tend to be larger and darker in color.

During the Pleistocene era in North America (a period that ran

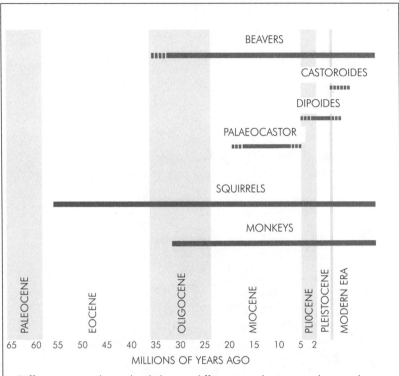

Different animals evolved during different geologic eras but evidence about the origin of rodents is more complex and doubtful than for most other kinds of mammals. Based on existing fossil records, beavers probably began to emerge as a distinct order early in the Oligocene, which began about 37 million years ago.

from about 1 million years to about 10,000 years ago), an earlier form of the modern beaver existed. Called the giant beaver (*Castoroides*), this animal was similar in shape to the beaver we are familiar with today, only much larger. Estimates made from fossilized bones indicate the giant beaver was about the size of the modern black bear, up to eight feet in length and more than 400 pounds (182 kg) in weight.

The tail of this enormous beaver was also impressive. Estimates based on the size of its tail vertebrae suggest a massive tail more than two feet long (65 cm) but not as proportionately wide as in the modern beaver, only six inches in width (14 cm).

Like the modern beaver, giant beavers had prominent incisors, up to six inches long (15 cm) with heavy ridges on the outside surface. The extra enamel in the ridges could have added strength to these outsized teeth, but some scientists think it may have been an adaptation for a different kind of grazing than is common with modern beavers. The molars of the giant beaver were also large in size, designed for efficient food-grinding activity, just like today's beavers and other herbivores.

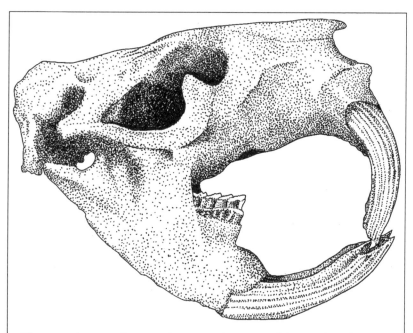

The giant beaver, *Castoroides*, a predecessor of the modern beaver, was much larger in size. Some fossilized specimens of this ancient rodent were as large as a black bear. This fossilized head features its oversized incisors, up to six inches long.

Giant beavers may not have been as dependent on the water as their modern cousins. Relatively short back legs and their massive size may have made them awkward swimmers. Their brain was about the only thing that was not over-sized. The brain of the giant beaver was about the same size as that found in beavers today.

Different kinds of beavers also existed during other eras in ancient times. More than twenty million years ago, an ancestor of the modern beaver called *Palaeocastor* lived in North America and dug burrows for its dens. During the Tertiary period, about 5 million years ago, a beaver-like animal called *Dipoides* had a range that extended through North America, most of Europe, and parts of western Asia. After the *Dipoides,* about 3 million years ago, a large pre-beaver called the *Procastoroides* was found. This animal could have been an early form of the giant beaver as it shares certain characteristics, including a large size. In Europe and Asia, another form of giant beaver called *Trogontherium* existed long before the modern European beaver arose.

When giant beavers roamed North America, it is believed that they covered most of the same range as modern beavers. Fossilized specimens have been found in a number of sites, from the Yukon south to Florida. Habitat that was suitable for these creatures was probably connected to major changes in the climate — extremes in temperature and precipitation — that altered the terrain and had a major effect on many kinds of vegetation.

During the ice age, giant beavers were still part of the wildlife. Remains have been found and dated to about 10,000 years ago, when the last glaciers extended deep into North America. The earliest forms of modern beavers have also been dated to this period, indicating that both forms lived at the same time.

While they thrived, giant beavers constructed lodges and burrows much like those of beavers today. But in accordance with this animal's larger size, these dwellings were also oversized. The preserved remnants of one giant beaver colony from what is now Ohio would have formed a lodge more than eight feet in diameter (2.4 m) and about four feet high (1.2 m). But there is no evidence that giant

45

beavers built dams and some experts believe that they may have thrived only because of the presence of natural lakes and swamps.

A few of the burrows that giant beavers constructed were preserved through sedimentation and other geological actions. These tunnels were not only large, but they were built in the form of corkscrews, spiralling into the ground. In some cases, the interior cavities were filled with mud or other debris, and over time, became petrified. As the outside ground eroded away, a spiral structure was left. These are called "devil's corkscrews."

When these structures were first sighted by settlers and explorers in the Great Plains in the late 1800s, they caused a great deal of puzzlement. For a time, people believed they were fused earth created by lightning strikes or the petrified root systems from bizarre ancient trees. In 1906, paleontologists discovered the fossil remains of a giant beaver at the bottom of one of the spirals, the first evidence that this animal existed.

TAXONOMY

"All the animals of which the industry has been the most vaunted, without excepting even the Ape with all that one can teach him, and all the others, are only that which they are, that is to say, beasts, in comparison with the Beaver, which passes only for a fish."

— Nicolas Denys (1672, *The Description and Natural History of the Coasts of North America*)

In the science of classification, taxonomists work to understand the relationship between plants and animals by defining their differences. In this scheme, beavers are classified as members of the rodent order, one of twenty-seven living orders of mammals and the largest group among all mammals. Among rodents, twenty-eight families and more than 2,000 different species are now recognized.

The Muridae family, representing most kinds of rats, mice, and voles, has 1,336 species and the Sciuridae, representing squirrels and chipmunks, has 272 species, but Castoridae, the family of beavers, is one of the smallest in the rodent order, having only two species. One is the beaver found in North America, whose taxonomic name is *Castor canadensis*, and the other is a similar-looking animal found in Europe, with the taxonomic name of *Castor fiber*.

Beavers are classified as rodents because like all animals in this order, they have two matching pairs of incisors at the front of their jaws, specialized teeth that keep growing throughout the life of the animal. Another characteristic of rodent teeth is a gap between the incisors in front and the teeth on the side where canine and premolar teeth are found in other mammal orders. The bone structure of rodent skulls is also unique, having developed to provide appropriate anchor points for the oversized muscles that go along with rodent jaws, the better to make use of their incisors as gnawing tools.

Other defining characteristics of rodents include two distinct bones in their lower arms, fur covering most of the body, and extended tails in a variety of forms.

The general structure of the skull and the design of the teeth not only differentiate rodents from other mammals, they are also used to organize rodents into two suborders, the Sciurognathi and the Hystricognathi. Beavers are grouped into the former, along with squirrels, rats, and pocket gophers; the latter includes porcupines, guinea pigs, and capybaras.

Rodents span a tremendous range in size. The smallest is the pygmy mouse, which is barely two inches in length (5 cm), and found in the southwestern United States south through central Mexico to Central America. The largest is the capybara, four feet long (1.2 m), and a resident of South America, found in Panama, Colombia, and south to Argentina. Next to capybaras, beavers are the second largest of all rodents and the largest on the North American continent.

Although taxonomists generally agree on what makes a specific kind of animal a certain species, they do not always agree on how to

SCIENTIFIC CLASSIFICATION

KINGDOM	• Animals
PHYLUM	• Chordata (vertebrates)
CLASS	• Mammalia (mammals)
ORDER	• Rodentia (rodents)
FAMILY	• Castoridae (beavers)
GENUS	• *Castor* (beavers)
SPECIES	• *Castor canadensis* (North American beaver) and *Castor fiber* (European beaver)

WORLD MAMMALS

ORDER	DESCRIPTION	No. of FAMILIES	No. of SPECIES
MONOTREMES	spiny anteaters, echidna	2	3
DIDELPHIMORPHIA	American opossums	4	66
PAUCITUBERCULATA	shrew opossums	1	7
MICROBIOTHERIA	monito del monte	1	1
DASYUROMORPHIA	carnivorous marsupials	3	64
PERAMELEMORPHIA	bandicoots	2	22
NOTORYCTEMORPHIA	marsupial mole	1	1
DIPROTODONTIA	koala, wombats, kangaroos	10	131
XENARTHRA	sloths, anteaters, armadillos	4	29
INSECTIVORA	hedgehogs, moles, shrews	7	440
SCANDENTIA	tree shrews	1	16
DERMOPTERA	flying lemurs	1	2
CHIROPTERA	bats	18	977
PRIMATES	monkeys, apes, lemurs	15	279
CARNIVORA	dogs, cats, bears, weasels	8	246
PINNIPEDIA	seals, walruses, sea lions	3	34
CETACEA	whales, dolphins, porpoises	13	78
SIRENIA	sea cow, manatees, dugong	2	4
PROBOSCIDEA	elephants	1	2
PERISSODACTYLA	horses, tapirs, rhinos	3	17
HYRACOIDEA	hyraxes	1	7
TUBULIDENTATA	aardvark	1	1
ARTIODACTYLA	pigs, hippos, giraffes, deer	10	221
PHOLIDOTA	pangolins	1	7
RODENTIA	rats, mice, squirrels, beaver	28	2,047
LAGOMORPHA	rabbits, hares, pikas	2	81
MACROSCELIDEA	elephant shrews	1	15

The classification shown here is from *Walker's Mammals of the World, Sixth Edition*. (1999, Johns Hopkins University Press)

WORLD RODENTS

FAMILY	DESCRIPTION	No. of GENERA	No. of SPECIES
APLODONTIDAE	mountain beaver	1	1
SCIURIDAE	squirrels, chipmunks	51	272
CASTORIDAE	beavers	1	2
GEOMYIDAE	pocket gophers	6	40
HETEROMYIDAE	pocket mice, kangaroo rats	6	60
DIPODIDAE	jumping mice, jerboas	17	51
MURIDAE	old world rats, voles, mice	301	1,336
ANOMALURIDAE	scaly-tailed squirrels	3	7
PEDETIDAE	springhaas	1	1
CTENODACTYLIDAE	gundis	4	5
MYOXIDAE	dormice	10	28
BATHYERGIDAE	African mole rats	5	14
HYSTRICIDAE	old world porcupines	3	11
PETROMURIDAE	dassie rat	1	1
THRYONOMYIDAE	cane rats	1	2
ERETHIZONTIDAE	new world porcupines	4	12
CHINCHILLIDAE	chinchillas, viscachas	3	6
DINOMYIDAE	pacarana	1	1
CAVIIDAE	cavies, guinea pigs, maras	5	17
HYDROCHOERIDAE	capybaras	1	1
DASYPROCTIDAE	agoutis	2	13
AGOUTIDAE	pacas	1	2
CTENOMYIDAE	tuco-tucos	1	48
OCTODONTIDAE	octodonts, degus	6	11
ABROCOMIDAE	chinchilla rats	1	5
ECHIMYIDAE	spiny rats, rock rats	19	73
CAPROMYIDAE	hutias	8	26
MYOCASTORIDAE	nutria	1	1

The classification shown here is from *Walker's Mammals of the World, Sixth Edition*. (1999, Johns Hopkins University Press)

WORLD RODENTS

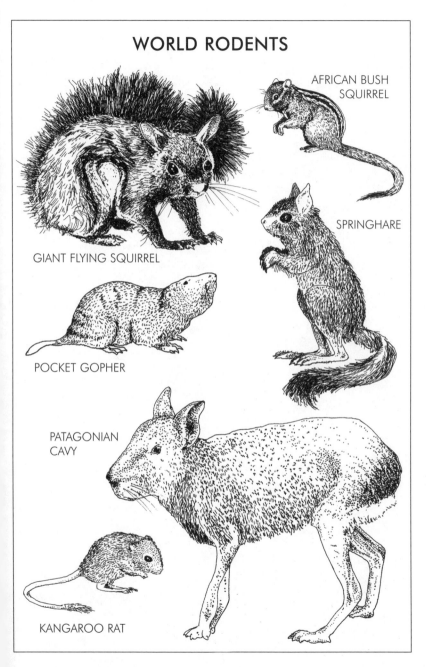

AFRICAN BUSH
SQUIRREL

GIANT FLYING SQUIRREL

SPRINGHARE

POCKET GOPHER

PATAGONIAN
CAVY

KANGAROO RAT

group species into families or suborders. With rodents, some taxonomists believe that instead of two suborders, there should be three. In past scientific eras, such distinctions were the basis of detailed ongoing research and discussion, basing the final organization on details of skeletal structure.

In the newest scientific era, now underway, taxonomists are increasingly turning to DNA analysis to establish links between species as well as crucial differences. The genetic material in Guinea pigs, for example, has been shown to be closer to that of rabbits, horses, and primates than to that of other rodents, but these native South American animals have not been reclassified because of this evidence, and may never be. Beavers, on the other hand, appear well-established as distinct members of the rodent order, their traditional taxonomic place as yet unchallenged.

RANGE

*"Over toward the far point where the lone pine stood,
I heard a faint splash and saw a spout of silver as a beaver
slapped its tail and dove, and then I followed the wake of
its swimming far toward the open, watched until it merged
with the sunlit ripples and was gone."*

— Sigurd F. Olson, (1958, "Beaver Cutting")

Once on the verge of extinction, beavers in North America are now rapidly expanding throughout most of their original range. This original range included almost every forested habitat from coast to coast and from the Gulf of Mexico north to the arctic. Although colonies existed in some parts of northern Mexico, the southern extent of this range was roughly the Rio Grande River in the west and the northern boundary of Florida in the east. In Utah, Arizona, and New Mexico, the range is limited to forested foothills and mountains. In California, the range is the northern two-thirds of the state, confined to the Sierra Nevada mountains and foothills.

In the south, beavers were not originally found in Florida except for the extreme northern part of the state and the panhandle. Along the Gulf coast, populations extend close to the shoreline except in the Mississippi Delta region, where their range ends 50 to 100 miles (80–160 km) from the shoreline.

To the north, beaver populations extended throughout Alaska except for the Arctic Slope, a band of territory from Point Hope east through the Yukon and Northwest Territory in Canada. Elsewhere in Canada, beavers were widely distributed south of the Arctic regions, including the Queen Charlotte Islands off the western coast of British Columbia and the islands around Newfoundland off the eastern coast.

Limits to the range of the beavers are determined by extreme cold and food supplies. They can survive, if not thrive, in areas without

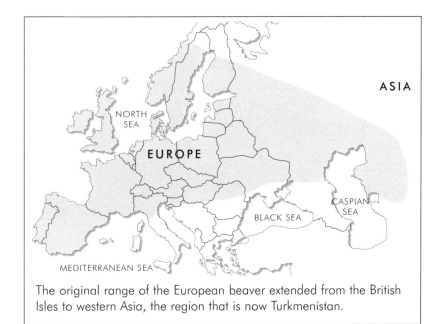

The original range of the European beaver extended from the British Isles to western Asia, the region that is now Turkmenistan.

heavy tree cover, but are most likely to be linked to dense stands of fast-growing trees in the willow and aspen families. Beavers have been found up to and beyond timberline in some regions, but are mostly tied to the natural range of willows and aspens, 9,000 to 10,000 feet in altitude at the high end.

In Europe, efforts have been ongoing to reintroduce beavers in many parts of their original range. This includes Russia, Germany, Poland, the Ukraine, France, and throughout Scandinavia. In the British Isles, plans are also underway to bring in colonies of beavers to replace native colonies that have been missing for a thousand years or more. This includes Scotland and Ireland. Beavers were still found in Scotland in the 1100s, and some indications point to small, scattered colonies in that country into the 1500s.

Their original range in Europe spanned the continent and extended into northern Asia and eastern Siberia. This included Scotland in the west, Mongolia in the southeast, northern Italy in the south, and Scandinavia and Siberia in the north.

BEAVER ANATOMY

"By using head, hands, teeth, tail, and webbed feet the beaver accomplishes much. The tail of a beaver is a useful and much-used appendage; it serves as a rudder, a stool, and a ramming or signal club."

— Enos A. Mills (1909, *Wild Life in the Rockies*)

Beaver bodies are large, a significant advantage for mammals that spend much time in the water. This is because there is a smaller ratio of surface area to body mass, improving the animal's ability to conserve heat. Beavers have a thick coat of specialized hair and a layer of fat underneath their skin, adaptations that protect against cold air as well as cold water. They have also evolved other specialized anatomy that aids in their water-based activities.

Webbed back feet enable strong propulsion; the large flat tail works as a rudder and counterbalance; and a rounded shape reduces water resistance. Like a few other mammals that spend a great deal of time in the water, the metabolism of beavers must perform extra duties in order to keep the animals from becoming chilled while wet. Before diving, for example, the body temperature of a beaver may increase by one or two degrees Fahrenheit. This extra temperature partially compensates for the coldness of the water, giving the animal a little extra time before chilling forces it onto land.

Although the beaver's body is designed for maximum efficiency in the water, the beaver spends less time in water than on land. In one measurement taken during winter conditions, adult beavers spent an average of two-and-a-half hours a day in the water, about 10 percent of a twenty-four hour period.

The shape of the beaver body, apparently ungainly on land, becomes an ally when in the water. The aerodynamic profile of this body shape has been measured as similar to that of some species of seals. The front feet, hind feet, and tail are the only areas of the

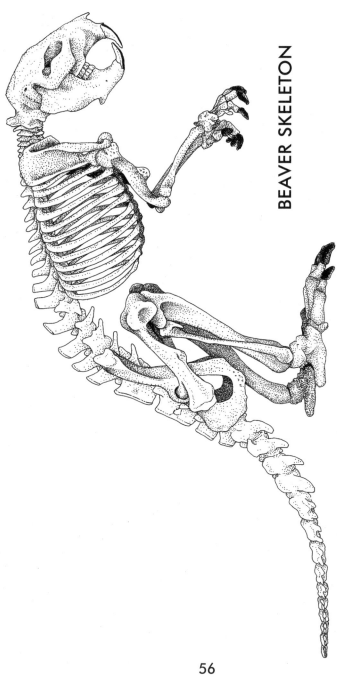

BEAVER SKELETON

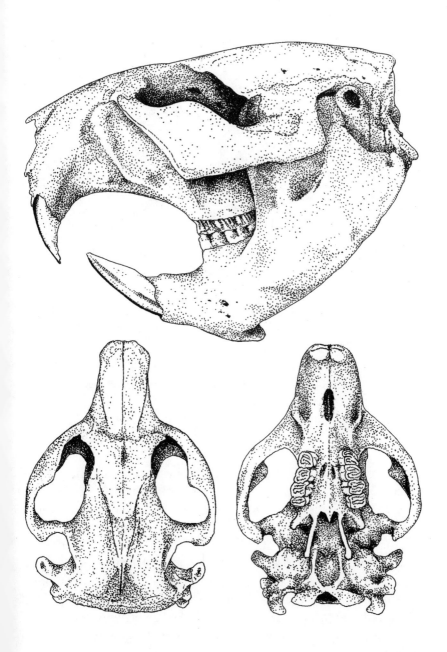

57

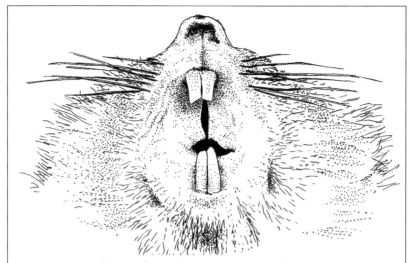

Beavers have flexible flaps of skin behind their front teeth. These flaps can be pulled together when a beaver is underwater, sealing the water out of its mouth and lungs and allowing the animal to use its teeth while submerged.

beaver body that are not heavily furred and comprise about 30 percent of its total surface area.

Beavers have other adaptations for efficient activity in the water. Their eyes have a protective layer called the nictitating membrane and the ears and nose have special inner flaps that seal out water. They are also able to gnaw underwater without swallowing water because of the specialized design of their mouths. Behind the incisors, their furred lips form a loose flap that closes behind these teeth, leaving them exposed for use but stopping water from entering the mouth. But they are also able to chew with their side teeth without swallowing water because the rear of the tongue can be raised, fitting tightly against the back of the mouth. Another unique breathing feature is the passage from their nose to their throat. This important airway connects directly to the upper lungs, permitting the beaver to chew and swallow, and breath through its nose at the same time.

FUR

The thick, heavy fur which encases the beaver gives it a remarkable advantage in its watery environment. This warm outer blanket also helps it survive in extremely cold weather. Unfortunately, it has also made beavers the target of humans, who covet the same qualities in fur.

Like many heavily furred mammals, beaver fur consists of two coats. An inner, or undercoat, consists of extremely fine, soft hairs that form a dense pile over the entire body except for the the feet and most of the tail. This undercoat is not only dense, the individual hairs cling together because of extremely tiny scales on their shafts. This rough outer edge helps mat the hairs of the undercoat together, trapping air. It also makes the undercoat of beaver fur valuable for making felt, as it creates a stronger bond than hair from

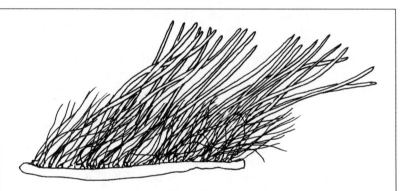

Beaver fur consists of two different kinds of hair. Longer, heavier outer hairs give the animal its color. Most beavers in North America are brown, but the brown tone can vary from light to dark. Beavers with very dark brown and black fur are also found, as are pale-colored and albino beavers. A denser undercoat of fine hair provides insulation. The undercoat also provides the material from which felt is made.

most other animals. The hair in the undercoat is a uniform color, usually gray.

Growing through the underfur are longer guard hairs that extend up and beyond the inner layer. In adult beavers, guard hairs are typically about two-and-one-half inches in length and these hairs are much thicker and coarser than the hairs found in the undercoat. The guard hairs on the back and sides are longer and often darker than those on the underside.

In healthy animals, guard hairs are normally shiny, a condition enhanced by the spreading of oil produced by oil glands. This is not the same fluid that is produced in the castor glands, but both sets of glands are found close together under the tail. According to people who have touched beavers who are in the water or still wet from the water, this hair has a slick, smooth feel to it, just the right texture for gliding through a wet environment.

During warm weather in spring or summer months, beavers molt, shedding only their guard hairs. They produce a replacement layer in time for winter, but the guard hairs are not fully grown until the peak of cold weather, usually in January or February.

The guard hairs contribute the defining color to the body. Each strand of guard hair is a uniform color. Guard hairs in North American beavers are typically brown, reddish-brown, yellowish-brown, or dark brown. Black beavers are common in some areas, and other color variations may include white or silver coats and some white beavers may be albinos. As with other albino mammals, the lack of color may affect the entire body or only segments, although the latter is a rare condition.

TEETH

The beavers' teeth are specialized tools well suited to their primary task, chewing through woody plant material. Like all rodents, the incisors grow constantly during the life of the animal. Use wears down the cutting surface, balancing the rate of growth. If they are not used, the incisors can grow too long, making it difficult or impossible for a beaver to eat and eventually causing it to die. A broken tooth can also have the same result, as the opposing tooth itself continues to grow out but without another surface to wear against, it grows so long that it prevents eating.

The cutting action of the incisors wears down the cutting surface at the same time that it keeps the edge sharp. This is because there are two materials in these teeth, a hard front enamel that forms the actual cutting edge and a softer material behind. The softer material is constantly abraded away by the action of gnawing. Adults sometimes exhibit "tooth sharpening" behavior by gnashing their front teeth together. Although this can be used as a threat display, it can also help to keep the cutting surfaces sharp.

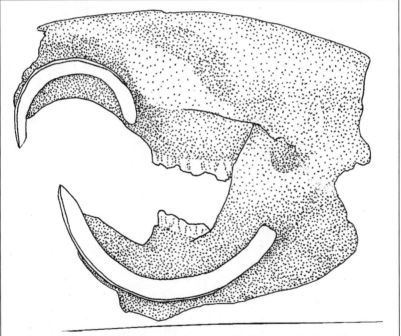

The incisors in beavers grow continuously throughout their life and must be used constantly in order to keep them from growing too long and causing health problems.

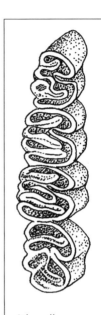

Like all rodents, beaver molars are designed to do an efficient job of grinding food into particles of digestible size.

Beavers have two prominent incisors in their upper jaw and two in their lower jaw, with the uppers overlapping the lowers. The enamel on the incisors is colored orange or yellow-orange on the front face.

Beavers develop tremendous cutting pressure with their teeth because of the unique shape of their skulls and the muscles attached to the jaw. These exert a powerful lever-action, at least twice as powerful as the jaw strength of humans.

The incisors in front do the cutting and molars on the sides are responsible for reducing food to digestible size. Beaver molars are uniquely shaped to grind wood into fibers. Grinding action includes both a back-to-front and side-to-side motion. Beavers also have pre-molars, one upper and one lower on each side, similar in size and shape to the molars. Like with all rodents, the canine teeth usually found between the premolars and incisors are missing, with a prominent gap in between.

EYES

Beavers have relatively small eyes and are not equipped with a very acute sense of vision. They rely more on their senses of smell and hearing to find food and detect danger. Although not acute, their vision is capable of detecting motion, a practical advantage in an animal that is prey to a variety of predators. Their vision is near-sighted, and they're better able to focus on objects close to them than those at a distance. One thing that their eyes do have is a special transparent eyelid, lacking in most other animals. This structure, called the nictitating membrane, closes across the outer surface of the eye whenever the beaver comes in contact with water. Its purpose is to protect the moist outer surface from being damaged or eroded by water, or particles suspended in the water. Thanks to this membrane, beavers can keep their eyes open under water, adding vision to their underwater activities.

EARS

Although small, beaver ears are capable of detecting small sounds from far away. Although little is known about the meaning of the various vocal sounds they make, the beaver's sense of hearing is clearly important in establishing and maintaining social structure. The auditory tubes are relatively large and end in auditory cavities that are larger than those in humans. These oversized organs help to pick up airborne sounds and in the water, detect water-borne sounds and vibrations that indicate danger. Because water is an efficient transmitter of sound, beavers may have a more effective ability to detect sounds that represent danger while in the water.

When on land, beaver ears may protrude from the head, helping to funnel sound into the hearing organs, but in the water, they lay down flat against the head to improve the animal's ability to swim and dive. To keep water out of the ear cavities, beavers have a specially adapted valve, a flap of skin that closes, forming an effective

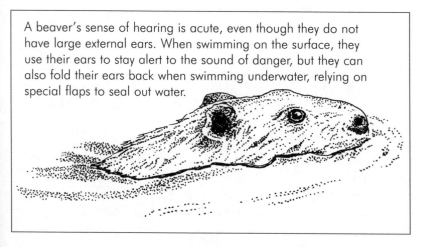

A beaver's sense of hearing is acute, even though they do not have large external ears. When swimming on the surface, they use their ears to stay alert to the sound of danger, but they can also fold their ears back when swimming underwater, relying on special flaps to seal out water.

seal when they are in the water. The position of the outer ears may also be used to provide nonverbal signals to other beavers.

NOSE

The beaver's sense of smell may be its most critical sense, helping it to find food, identify members of its colony, and detect beavers who are strangers. The nose, a highly sensitive organ in beavers, can also provide advance warning of prey animals. Beavers use their noses to select food and are attracted to plant sources by aroma, even though final selection may include factors such as distance from the water and size, as in the diameter of a tree trunk.

The sense of smell is an important factor in identifying and protecting territory, a sense based on the unique chemical characteristics of the castoreum produced by the beavers' castor glands. Beavers are able to differentiate between the castoreum produced by members of their own families and that produced by beavers in neighboring territories.

Upon exiting their lodges or burrows, beavers often swim in circles while they sniff the air, using their sense of smell to detect potential threats. When they leave the water to feed, some observers report that they are more likely to choose the upwind bank, behavior that also may be linked to their reliance on smell.

FEET AND LEGS

Beavers are unique among rodents because they are the only animals in this order to have five digits on each foot. Their front feet in particular are extremely sensitive and dextrous, giving them the ability to feel for food and building materials in murky underwater conditions and in the dark. Beavers can grasp branches or other objects in their front paws because one of the outside fingers works almost like the opposing thumb in primates.

The rear legs and feet are much larger than the front. The length of the adult rear foot is six to seven inches and, unlike the rest of its body, the beaver's rear feet do not have fur. All five digits on each foot are equipped with long, sturdy claws, which are useful appendages for digging and grasping.

The claws on the front paws are about an inch long and pointed; claws on the rear feet are shorter and less pointed. Strong and durable, these claws function as efficient digging tools in various activities, such as excavating burrows and canals.

A unique feature that is found on the first two digits of the rear feet is a unique double claw, sometimes called a split nail. Here, a thin second nail lies closely next to a larger main nail or horny pad, creating a narrow slit. Beavers are able to move these double claws

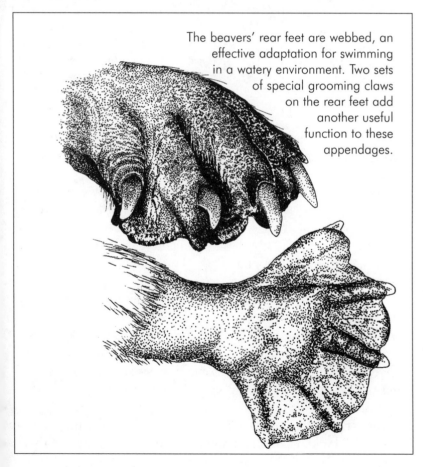

The beavers' rear feet are webbed, an effective adaptation for swimming in a watery environment. Two sets of special grooming claws on the rear feet add another useful function to these appendages.

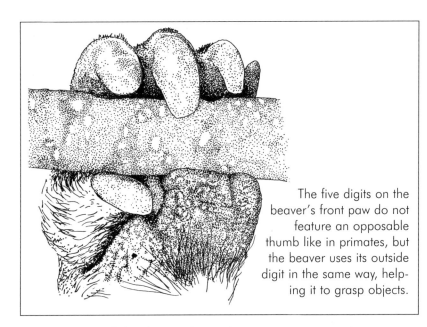

The five digits on the beaver's front paw do not feature an opposable thumb like in primates, but the beaver uses its outside digit in the same way, helping it to grasp objects.

like a clamp and this feature has at least one important function — it gives a beaver added efficiency when combing and grooming its fur.

Some biologists also believe the double claw may have evolved in response to one type of beaver parasite, a large beetle that lives in its fur. In grooming, the beaver pulls its double nails along sections of its guard hairs, smoothing and straightening them and at the same time, removing dirt and debris. This action also helps spread oil over the fur, helping repel water.

The two sets of double nails differ slightly in construction. The inner nail is larger and rougher along the edge, forming what beaver experts call a "coarse comb." The outer nail is smaller and has a finer, minutely serrated edge. This nail is called a "fine comb." Although designed to comb fur, some beavers have been observed using one of these nails to remove wood chips and splinters that have been wedged between its front teeth.

Although the front feet are in constant use during feeding, walking on land, building, and grooming, the beaver does not use them

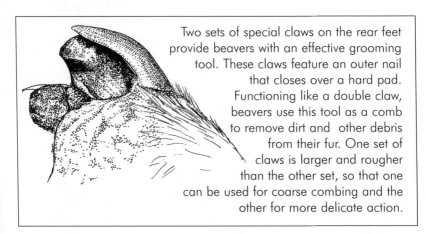

Two sets of special claws on the rear feet provide beavers with an effective grooming tool. These claws feature an outer nail that closes over a hard pad. Functioning like a double claw, beavers use this tool as a comb to remove dirt and other debris from their fur. One set of claws is larger and rougher than the other set, so that one can be used for coarse combing and the other for more delicate action.

when swimming. When diving or swimming, the front feet are tucked in close to the chest and propulsion is provided by the powerful kicking action of the webbed rear feet.

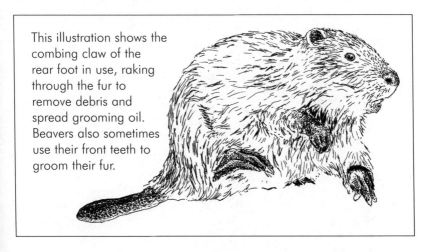

This illustration shows the combing claw of the rear foot in use, raking through the fur to remove debris and spread grooming oil. Beavers also sometimes use their front teeth to groom their fur.

TAIL

The tail is the signature characteristic of the beaver, and is well-designed to supplement its activities. Broad and flat, the tail is almost hairless and covered with a layer of dark, tough skin. Adult tails are 10 to 18 inches in length (25–45 cm) and 4 to 5 inches in width (10–13 cm), with a thickness of one-half to one inch in the middle (1.3–2.5 cm). The tail will grow in length and width during its lifetime but after the beaver reaches maturity at three to four years of age, it doesn't grow much. During the course of a year, however, the beaver's diet and food intake may add some temporary thickness as food is converted to fat and stored in the tail.

The furred portion of its body extends into the base end of the tail for about one quarter of the length of the tail. The rest of the tail surface is covered with dark, leathery skin that has the appearance of scales, but they are not true scales like those of fish, but a scale-like pattern of ridges on the surface of the skin. Although mostly hairless, a few scattered strands are present. The center of the tail is an extension of the spine, consisting of flattened bones called caudal vertebrae, that are similar to the bones in most rodent tails.

The tissue in the tail is a fatty substance that is important to the beaver as a source of stored energy in times of food shortage. The network of blood vessels in the tail also helps the beaver control its

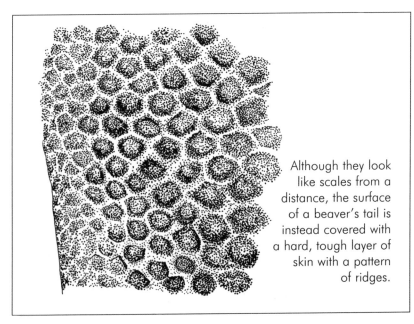

Although they look like scales from a distance, the surface of a beaver's tail is instead covered with a hard, tough layer of skin with a pattern of ridges.

body temperature, radiating excess heat when it is too warm and limiting heat loss when the outside temperature is too cold.

In use, the tail is relatively flexible. In the water, it mainly serves as a rudder, helping beavers to maintain or change direction. On land, it forms a sturdy base, creating a stable tripod in conjunction with the two hind legs when beavers are standing to gnaw on trees, a common activity. There are some ligaments and muscles in the tail, mostly near the base, that give the tail some usefulness as a leverage device when dragging or pulling branches.

Beavers also rely on their tails to create loud slaps on the surface of the water, the standard beaver alarm. But despite this functionality, beavers do not use their tails in their construction activities, even though some beaver myths claim that their tails are essential tools for applying mud to the surface of their lodges and dams.

GLANDS

Beavers are equipped with a pair of specialized scent glands. These organs, called the castor glands, emit a strong-smelling liquid called castoreum, an important biological element used by beavers to mark their territories. The castor glands are located near their anus and they discharge castoreum through the anus. Castor glands are large, measuring about four inches long in adults.

The liquid is typically orange, yellowish-orange, or deep yellow in color, and is produced by both sexes. The castor glands in male beavers, however, are usually larger than those in females. Some wildlife biologists believe that the castoreum produced by each sex is different in color and viscosity, one of the few differences between males and females.

Analysis of castoreum reveals that individuals in the same family share some of the same chemical markers, one of the reasons that family members can recognize one another as well as detect the presence of strangers.

Both sexes have a second set of glands, located near the castor glands, that secretes a specialized oil through a single opening called the cloaca, discharging into the anus. This compound is a critical

INTERNAL ARRANGEMENT OF GLANDS

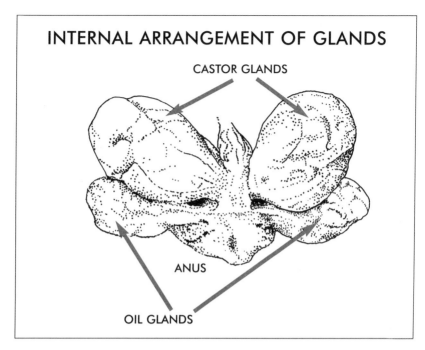

CASTOR GLANDS

ANUS

OIL GLANDS

element in grooming and keeping their fur waterproof. The oil discharges through pores into the skin near the anus, where it is picked up and spread with the front feet.

When it is in a typical grooming posture, a beaver appears to be sitting on its tail. This is not to keep its fur dry and out of contact with the ground, but because it is the most effective position for the animal to gain access to its supply of grooming oil, exuded from the anus, located under the tail and between its rear legs.

Sitting upright on its tail, a beaver has access to the oil secreted from its oil glands. This oil is different from that secreted by the castor glands, which is used for marking its territory.

REPRODUCTION

"The Indians think the Male and Female are faithful to each other, they bring up their young for the first year with care and protection, until the next spring when the female is about to litter she drives them all away, and some of them, before they can be made to stay away, receive severe cuts on the back from the teeth of the old ones."

— David Thompson (1784–1812, *David Thompson's Narrative of His Exploration in Western America*)

Male and female beavers are virtually identical in size, color, and shape. Unlike most other mammals, there are no external differences in sexual organs that could be used to tell them apart. In fact, beaver sexes are nearly identical internally as well. Each has a single opening in the rear, the anus, a combination orifice for both defecation and other functions. Females have four mammary glands and four teats, but these are normally inconspicuous, visible only when a mother is nursing young.

Internally, many, but not all, male beavers have been found to have a rudimentary uterus, similar to that in the females. These are non-functioning organs and may occur as a normal genetic characteristic or as a result of environmental influences, such as the presence of chemicals in water supplies. The penis and testicles of the male beaver are hidden inside the urogenital passage and the penis has an internal bone, about an inch and a half long.

Female beavers have a short period of estrus, or "heat," during which they are receptive to mating. The initial estrus period lasts from ten to twelve hours and if the mating does not result in fertilized eggs, another period of estrus will occur a few weeks later. In the southern part of its range, beavers may mate as early as December or even late November, but elsewhere, mating occurs from January to March. The colder the climate, the later the mating.

BEAVER SIZE

Adult beavers are found in a wide range of sizes, with the largest typically found farther to the north of their natural range. Most beavers continue to put on weight as they age, although most of their growth happens before they are four years old. The largest known beaver was a specimen captured in 1938 in Wyoming. This massive beaver weighed 115 pounds. Other beavers have been found with weights of 90 to 96 pounds, but the average weight for most adults is between 40 and 60 pounds, with both sexes about the same size. When born, beaver kits usually weigh about 1 pound. At six weeks, the average weight is about

NEWBORN

ONE MONTH

4 pounds and at one year old, they weigh between 10 and 15 pounds. Yearlings, adolescents between the ages of one and two, weigh 20 to 25 pounds. Two-year-olds weigh 30 to 35 pounds.

YEARLING

BEAVER LIFESPAN

Beavers can live to be 10 to 12 years old in the wild, on average. Some specimens in the wild have been estimated to be much older, up to 24 years old. In captivity, beavers typically live for more than 20 years, with the oldest known beaver living to be 50 years old in a zoo.

Mating between beavers generally occurs in the water. The beaver is one of few mammals that copulates front to front, usually with the male on the top, but they also use the more standard animal mating position, with the male mounting the female from behind.

The gestation period for females is thought to be about 120 days, but reports vary from as little as 98 days to as long as 128 days. The gestation period may vary according to latitude and climate. Females produce litters of one to nine young, called kits. The typical size of a litter is four or five, with older, more experienced beaver mothers often producing larger litters. Larger litters are also more common in locations where there are abundant sources of food trees.

Beaver populations, in fact, may be somewhat regulated by the availability of food, with ample stands of desirable trees and lack of competition or predation increasing beaver numbers. In colonies of beavers studied over long periods of time, not all the adult females give birth every year, contributing to a population size more in balance with its habitat.

In most of their range in North America, female beavers have a single litter per year. But in the extreme southern part of this range, there are reports of females having more than one litter, the second coming in late summer or early fall. This adaptation is probably linked to the weather conditions found in warmer climates, with food supplies less diminished during the winter.

Beaver babies are born with a coat of fur already in place and their eyes partially open. Young typically weigh from 14 to 18 ounces (400 to 510 gms) and are 12 to 15 inches in length (30–38 cm) at birth. Young beavers, called kits, begin nursing within the first hour or so after birth and rapidly put on weight.

The young also arrive equipped with partially emerged front teeth, but like other mammals, they are totally dependent on their mother's milk for at least several weeks. Kits may start nibbling and ingesting solid food while they are still in the suckling phase, which lasts one to two months. Kits suckle up to nine times a day, usually a few minutes to ten minutes at a time.

Young beavers stay inside the lodge or burrow for the first few months of their lives. They are active and move around within a few days of birth. They may begin swimming when they are only a few weeks old, but mostly within the confines of the lodge tunnels. One observer has reported a beaver kit swimming when it was only one day old. Although the influence of their mother and other relatives can provide important knowledge to young beavers, swimming is one thing that is purely instinct and even orphaned kits take to the water without coaxing. In the water, the beaver kits are so buoyant they are unable to dive under the surface.

As they begin to eat solid food, their meals are brought to the denning chamber by the mother, both parents, or other family members. The kits will also begin gnawing at an early age even if they don't eat what they gnaw, driven by the instinct to wear down the ever-growing incisor teeth.

Beavers live in extended families, often with three generations in a single colony. The newborns share space with the adolescents from the previous year and the young adults who have yet to leave the nest and start their own families. While the mother beaver is preparing to give birth, however, she often chases adolescents and the father beaver out of the denning area and they may be banned for one or more weeks after the birth.

Young beavers are too small to be of much use to the colony for their first year of life, but they often accompany family members on forages for food and in their dam maintenance activities. More so than most other rodents, young beavers spend a lot of time playing, chasing each other and frolicking in general.

Beavers may be ready to mate before they are two years old but most do not begin mating until after their second year. In some cases, breeding may be delayed until the third or fourth year.

Beaver colonies can range in size from two to ten or more, but five or six is the most common number. All of the extended family members help feed and protect the young as well as participate in the building and repair of lodges and dams. Females as well as males help maintain communal scent markers and are active in defending their territory against beavers from outside. Females, in fact, often lead the way when it comes to many beaver construction activities and are much more active than males in issuing alarms — tail slaps — when danger threatens.

At the end of their first year of growth, young beavers usually weigh 25 pounds or more. In another year, their weight can increase to as much as 40 or 45 pounds and by the third year, adult weights of 50 pounds or more are typical. Some studies have suggested that most adult beavers continue growing in size and weight as they get older, although the rate of growth slows considerably after the first few years.

BEAVER FOOD

"Certainly in the beaver God has given a remarkable gift to this new country, a gift which other nations are so anxious to share; for there is perhaps no animal that is more wonderful."

— Father François du Creux (1664, *History of Canada or New France*)

Beavers have thrived throughout much of their natural history because of an ability to take advantage of a unique food niche. Although many other kinds of animals can digest cellulose, beavers are more dependent on it than most. Beavers are able to digest about 30 to 35 percent of the cellulose contained in the woody material they ingest, partly because of digestive secretions in their stomach and partly because of colonies of digestive bacteria that are found in their gut. They also have a long and extended lower digestive system that has evolved to handle the woody material that passes through it. Porcupines, another mammal able to digest wood, also have specialized lower digestive systems, but the lower intestine in the beaver is 70 percent longer than that of the porcupine.

Beavers sometimes run the same food through their system more than once, increasing the amount of nutrients extracted. They do this through the process of coprophagy, the act of eating their own feces. What's left over is unique — scat that resembles small balls

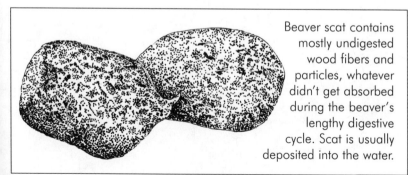

Beaver scat contains mostly undigested wood fibers and particles, whatever didn't get absorbed during the beaver's lengthy digestive cycle. Scat is usually deposited into the water.

THE TREE LARDER

Beavers eat the inner bark (cambium) and outer bark of many kinds of trees, but they also use other parts of trees for food, including leaves, twigs, roots, shoots, buds, flowers, catkins, acorns and other seeds, nuts, fruit, and tree sap.

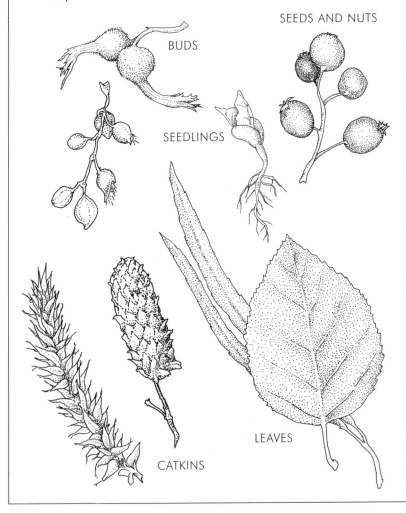

SEEDS AND NUTS

BUDS

SEEDLINGS

LEAVES

CATKINS

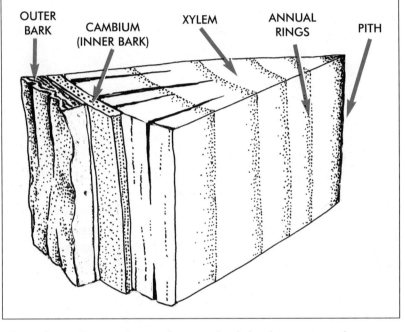

TREE ANATOMY

Except for very small or young trees, beavers typically target the inner bark and sometimes the outer bark, depending on the species of tree.

OUTER BARK

CAMBIUM (INNER BARK)

XYLEM

ANNUAL RINGS

PITH

of sawdust, almost always deposited while they are in the water. Beavers do not deposit scat inside their lodges.

How much do beavers eat? Adult beaver diets range from about one pound (.5 kg) to five and one-half pounds (2.5 kg) of woody material a day. In general, beavers eat from one to two pounds of food per day. In the summer months, they often eat more plant material than trees and in some locations only target trees in the late summer and fall.

When felling trees just for food, a single beaver averages about one tree every other night. Aspen trees, the favored food source throughout much of their range, can provide enough food for an adult beaver for a single day when one to two inches in diameter, or about the size of a six-year-old tree. If a tree is used for food, beavers usually only target its smaller branches, leaves, and bark. With trees of two to three inches in diameter, beavers may consume from 50 to 90 percent of the part of the tree that is cut down.

When foraging on aspens, beavers average two to four pounds of aspen bark daily (1–1.8 kg) and a single adult beaver can consume up to 200 aspen trees in a year. In most of their range, bark, leaves, and woody material from trees provide their entire diet during winter months, but only half or less during non-winter periods.

Although most people think of the beaver as an eater of trees, this is something of a cliché. Trees typically provide the bulk of the diet for the majority of beavers in most areas but they are fairly liberal when it comes to food sources, as long as they are vegetarian, as they also consume water plants, grasses, and even farm crops. And when they focus on trees, they are also very general about what they eat. They will eat the inner bark, the outer bark, inner sapwood, larger trunks, saplings, roots, shoots, buds, leaves, seeds, and flowers as well. But what they prefer most of the time is the leaves and the newest layer of bark, called the cambium, found just underneath the outer bark.

The beaver diet points toward clear preferences when it comes to trees. Not just in species, but size. In general, they avoid larger trees unless there is little else to eat in an area. The ideal tree size for most beavers is a diameter of a few inches. This is not necessarily because such young trees are tastier or more nutritious, but quicker to fell. For beavers, time spent on land is a threat to their survival, pointing them toward trees that take the least time to turn into food.

For the same reason, beavers rarely travel farther than necessary to find a suitable tree for felling, again because of the danger. Trees are rarely eaten at the site where they are felled, but carried or dragged to the water. At the height of the growth season for trees, these downed trees may be consumed the same day, or dragged to underwater caches for later use.

Fast-growing trees are the most typical part of the beaver diet. This primarily includes aspen, poplar, and willow, species that also are quick to regrow, often sprouting from the cut-off sections of trunk. In different parts of the continent, beavers will take advantage of local herbaceous plants and are not likely to pass up any tree if it represents the only meal around. Throughout their range, conifers are not targeted as often as non-conifers and in some areas, are avoided completely. Trees that are dead are also avoided, as this kind of vegetable matter provides little or no nutrition, at least to beavers, but they may gnaw on or fell dead trees to use in constructing lodges or dams.

How do beavers select which trees to eat? They have highly developed senses of smell and taste and usually pick a species for its preferred taste, but sometimes the size of the tree and its distance from the water can influence their choice. Beavers that have been captured and offered precut selections of more than one kind of tree can be picky, eating them in order beginning with the ones they think taste best. In one test, quaking aspen was the clear winner.

Beavers may have evolved their taste preferences to match the nutritional value of the trees that were available to them. In taste tests, beavers have been shown to select trees that provide the greatest long-term energy intake.

When there are plenty of trees around to choose from, beavers will perform "taste tests," sampling the bark on a tree to determine if it meets their standards. If they don't like what they taste, they move on to the next tree. In the fall, beavers have also been observed "girdling" trees before cutting them down. This action consists of removing the bark in a ring around the circumference of the trunk, stopping the sap from flowing through the bark. Girdled trees will eventually die, but biologists believe there is a different motive at work with beavers. They may be preparing a tree for storage underwater by letting the bark dry out before cutting. Beavers have been observed girdling a number of trees of similar size during a single night, then returning a few days to a week later to fell them, carrying the resulting forage to underwater caches.

TREE MENU

Trees in North America that beavers are known to target as food include ...

alder, Arizona alder, Arroyo willow, ash, aspen, balsam poplar, balsam willow, Bebb willow, beech, black cottonwood, black oak, black willow, box elder, canyon maple, cherry, chinaberry, dogwood, eastern cottonwood, feltleaf willow, Fremont cottonwood, gray birch, hickory, Hinds willow, holly, hornbeam, ironwood, juniper, littletree willow, loblolly pine, Lombardy poplar, Mackenzie willow, mountain alder, narrowleaf cottonwood, Northwest willow, Pacific willow, paper birch (white birch), pecan, plains cottonwood, peachleaf willow, pussy willow, quaking aspen, red alder, red birch, red maple, red oak, sandbar willow, silver bells, silver maple, Sitka alder, speckled alder, spruce pine, sugar berry, sweet bay, sweetgum, sycamore, tupelo gum, water birch, wax myrtle, white alder, white poplar, wild grapevine, witch hazel, yaupon

Favorite tree food sources are ...

Poplars (balsam poplar, black cottonwood, eastern cottonwood, Fremont cottonwood, narrowleaf cottonwood, quaking aspen, plus introduced species)

Willows (balsam willow, Bebb willow, black willow, feltleaf willow, Hinds willow, littletree willow, Mackenzie willow, Northwest willow, Pacific willow, peachleaf willow, pussy willow, sandbar willow, Sitka willow, plus introduced species)

Birches (Arizona alder, mountain alder, paper birch, red alder, Sitka alder, speckled alder, yellow birch, water birch, white alder)

The sharp, prominent incisors in the beaver's mouth are its principal tool for turning trees into food. They will often remove a branch or piece of trunk that is a manageable length, hold it in their front feet, and strip the bark away as they rotate the piece, similar to how human picnickers attack an ear of corn. Most branches they select are eaten only down to the pith or sapwood, then discarded. With limbs of narrow diameter, they can also attack their food from the end, diminishing it like a stalk of celery.

Beavers may be efficient lodge and dam builders, but they are noted for their sloppy eating habits. For one thing, they create almost as much waste as they consume. Large trees, for example, are usually felled only to remove the leaves and smaller branches. Some trees are targeted only for their bark, leaving the rest to decay. A few trees, such as the sweet gum found in the southern states, attract them only because of a fragrant sap, which they consume while ignoring the rest of the tree. And while they are chomping away, they spill and scatter large and small pieces of bark, twigs, leaves, and branches.

Around their favorite eating sites, which are often clearings on a bank or near their lodges, piles of pencil-sized sticks may by strewn, leftover cores from the stripping operations of their teeth. These discarded remnants may also float on the surface of a beaver pond, an indication of its active inhabitants. Cores that sink to the bottom can form a distinctive layer of underwater litter. Not one to waste woody material, however, beavers sometime recycle these chewed-over bits, adding them to the framework of their lodges and dams. And in times of food shortages, this discarded woody debris may be sought out for additional eating.

In southern states, beavers are often found in habitats with a greater variety of trees than in the northern part of their range. Here, their choice of trees is more likely to include hardwoods, such as oak and maple. Other southern favorites are known to include dogwood, tupelo gum, sweet bay, juniper, pecan, elm, hornbeam, chinaberry, box elder, holly, and wax myrtle.

In general, beavers have been observed targeting many more tree species in southern regions than in the north. At the extreme northern part of their range and at high altitudes, they may feed only on aspen or willow. In the southern extremes, their diet may include two to three dozen tree species within a single colony's territory.

Throughout much of their North American range, the aspen tree shares a similar ecosystem with beavers. Because aspens are the most widely distributed tree on the continent, their life cycle has a

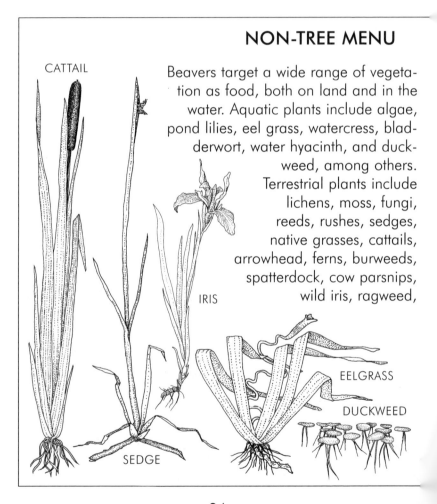

NON-TREE MENU

CATTAIL

Beavers target a wide range of vegetation as food, both on land and in the water. Aquatic plants include algae, pond lilies, eel grass, watercress, bladderwort, water hyacinth, and duckweed, among others. Terrestrial plants include lichens, moss, fungi, reeds, rushes, sedges, native grasses, cattails, arrowhead, ferns, burweeds, spatterdock, cow parsnips, wild iris, ragweed,

IRIS

EELGRASS

DUCKWEED

SEDGE

close connection with beavers. In one year, a single beaver can consume up to 200 aspens if that is their primary source of food in an area, and cut all of the aspens within 400 feet of the water's edge.

When beavers become active in the spring, aspens have their highest protein value, helping to compensate for the nutritional losses during the winter. And aspens are about the first trees to begin growing in the spring. This is because the litter that accumulates under them during the course of the year decays rapidly, pro-

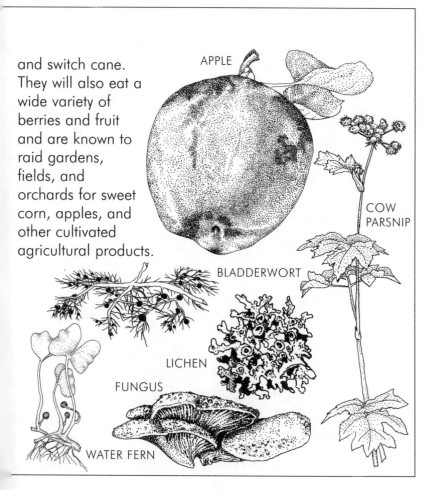

and switch cane. They will also eat a wide variety of berries and fruit and are known to raid gardens, fields, and orchards for sweet corn, apples, and other cultivated agricultural products.

APPLE

COW PARSNIP

BLADDERWORT

LICHEN

FUNGUS

WATER FERN

viding a rich bed of humus, nurturing new growth. This litter is typically thicker than that found under stands of other kinds of trees that grow among aspens, particularly conifers.

During the winter months, the litter acts as insulation, keeping the soil moist underneath. The bare branches of aspens also permit more sun to reach the ground, melting snow faster in the spring than in other kinds of tree stands. The combination of these factors help aspens respond quickly at the beginning of the growing season, giving them an advantage over other tree species, and at the same time making them an abundant source of food just when beavers need it.

Aspens produce seeds as a way to generate new trees but in many parts of their range, particularly in the west and north, underground roots are the primary source of new growth. In some cases, groves of aspens are all interconnected, clones growing from the same root system. One such aspen grove in Utah covers more than 17 acres and consists of an estimated 47,000 trees. Aspen groves in the east usually live for only 50 to 60 years, but in the west, groves can survive for up to 150 years.

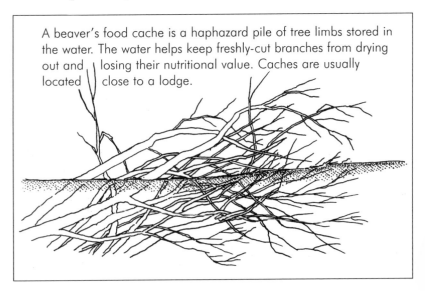

A beaver's food cache is a haphazard pile of tree limbs stored in the water. The water helps keep freshly-cut branches from drying out and losing their nutritional value. Caches are usually located close to a lodge.

Aspens are among the first trees to regenerate after a forest fire. In the first six to ten years, groves spread quickly, but individual trees are not long-lived. The litter and rich soil produced by this growth hinders their continuing growth, favoring new trees over old. In the ecosystem of the aspen, long term growth of the grove creates a continual replacement of old trees by new ones. Both fires and beavers are a natural part of this cycle.

The cottonwood is a type of tree that responds to injury or cutting by sending out new sprouts, and beavers are an important factor in creating new cottonwood growth. Natural chemicals, called phenolic glycosides, are produced to protect the tree against animals that try to eat it. These chemicals form a natural protection by being distasteful and even toxic to most animals. The chemicals are produced in higher concentrations in regrowth tissue — sprouts that grow in response to injury or cutting. Here, the trees have concentrated their defense in response to a threat to their survival.

Biologists have noted that the protective chemicals seem to be most effective against animals that graze on a wide variety of plants. Hares, for example, are known to avoid sprouts and young growth in cottonwood trees, but will feed on more mature trees. Beavers, on the other hand, target the cottonwood tree as a major source of food and seem to have developed a resistance to this chemical, preferring the young growth over more mature parts of these trees.

Certain species of leaf beetles have also developed a taste for the new cottonwood growth and have developed a resistance to the chemical protection. These beetles in turn may be protected from predators because their digestive systems convert the chemicals into other toxins that are even more powerful.

In southern states or wherever there are mild winter conditions, beavers may forage for food throughout the winter. But throughout most of their range, cold and ice common to the winter months are accompanied by caching behavior, the gathering and storage of food for leaner times.

Food storage in beaver ponds or streams consists of individual leafy branches or lengths of edible trees stashed underwater, wedged

FOOD TREE PROFILE: ASPEN

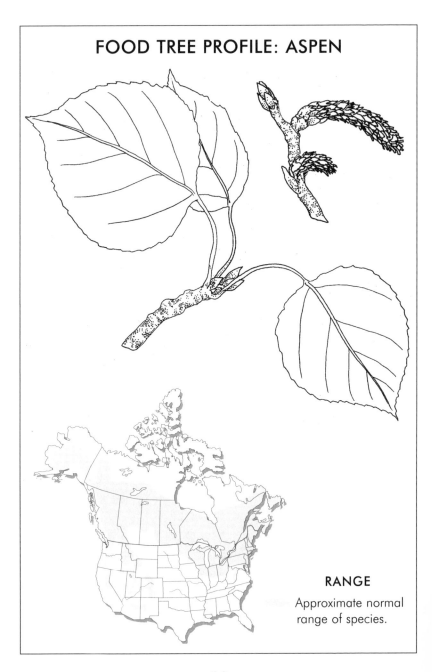

RANGE

Approximate normal range of species.

FOOD TREE PROFILE

NAME

Aspen (quaking aspen, trembling aspen)
Populus tremuloides

DESCRIPTION

Fast growing deciduous tree. Thin, light-colored bark, ovately-shaped leaf with rounded base and finely serrated edge, fuzzy tufted catkins. Leaves green on top, dull green on underside; leaves yellow to golden in fall. Reproduces from seeds and clones itself from root system. Often short-lived, colonies sprout in open areas, succeeded by conifers or hardwoods.

FOOD SOURCE

Bark, leaves, and shoots browsed by beavers, deer, elk, moose, sheep, goats, and rabbits. Buds browsed by grouse, quail, squirrels, and other small mammals.

SIZE

Maximum 70 feet high. Average 30–40 feet high. Trunk diameter 3–16 inches. Leaves 1–3 inches long. Growth to 6–24 inches by end of first year.

RANGE AND HABITAT

Most widely distributed tree in North America. Present throughout most of Canada, in all states except those in the southeast, and in northern Mexico. Grows at sea level up to 11,500 feet; found in northern range only to about 3,000 feet; found in Mexico primarily above 8,000 feet. In different parts of range either on south, southwestern, or northern exposures. Grows in several kinds of soil; prefers sandy or gravelly conditions. Common around standing water, streams, and rivers, on gentle slopes, moist upland woods, mesas and plateaus, dry mountainsides, valley bottoms, and talus. Dies off in response to waterlogging.
Common in habitats of spruce-fir, pine, and mixed hardwoods.

FOOD TREE PROFILE: COTTONWOOD

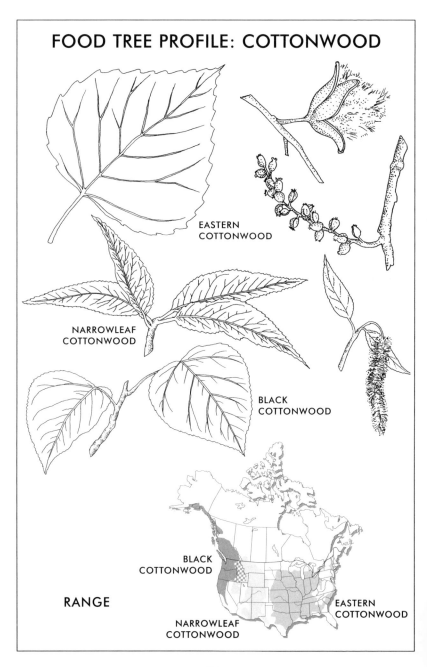

EASTERN
COTTONWOOD

NARROWLEAF
COTTONWOOD

BLACK
COTTONWOOD

BLACK
COTTONWOOD

RANGE

EASTERN
COTTONWOOD

NARROWLEAF
COTTONWOOD

FOOD TREE PROFILE

NAME	**Cottonwood** *Populus deltoides* (eastern); *Pop. anfustifolia* (narrowleaf); *Pop. trichocarpa* (black)
DESCRIPTION	Fast growing deciduous tree. Smooth, light-colord bark when young; darker and fissured when older; leaves oval to lance-shaped with serrated edges; seed pods with characteristic "cotton." Leaves green on top, lighter underside; yellow in fall. Reproduces from seeds, resprouts from stumps.
FOOD SOURCE	Bark, leaves, and shoots browsed by beavers, deer, elk, moose, sheep, goats, and rabbits. Buds browsed by grouse, quail, squirrels, and other small mammals.
SIZE	Eastern: 80–100 feet. Trunk diameter 4–6 feet. Leaves 4–5 inches. Narrowleaf: 50–60 feet. Trunk diameter 1–2 feet. Leaves 2–4 inches. Black: 60–120 feet. Trunk diameter 1–3 feet. Leaves 3–6 inches.
RANGE AND HABITAT	Eastern found in lowlands and valleys; narrowleaf most commonly found from 3,500–8,000 feet; black from sea level–7,000 feet. Prefers gentle slopes and bottomland near streams and rivers. Eastern cottonwood found 15–20 feet above level of stream; narrowleaf found 1.5–6 feet above water line. Grows in several kinds of soil; prefers sandy or silty conditions. Dies off in response to waterlogging. Eastern associated with black ash/American elm/red maple forests; narrowleaf and black often found with willows. Black cottonwood is largest hardwood in West.

FOOD TREE PROFILE: POPLAR

RANGE

Approximate normal
range of species.

FOOD TREE PROFILE

NAME	**Balsam Poplar** (balm, tacamahac) *Populus balsamifera*
DESCRIPTION	Fast growing deciduous tree. Leaves slightly oval and pointed with edges finely serrated. Leaf color green to dark green; lighter color underneath. Bark tan or light brown with smooth texture when young; with age, bark turns gray and develops ridges. Buds have distinctive odor of balsam. Reproduces from seeds, clones itself from root system, and also resprouts from stumps.
FOOD SOURCE	Bark and shoots browsed by beavers, deer, elk, moose, sheep, goats, and rabbits. Buds browsed by grouse, quail, squirrels, and other small mammals.
SIZE	Maximum 100 feet high. Average 40–50 feet high. Trunk diameter 1–3 feet. Leaves 3–5 inches long.
RANGE AND HABITAT	Found farther to the north than any other hardwood in North America. Favors higher elevations, with stands found up to 6,000 feet in lower Rocky Mountains. Stands develop dominance at a site within 15 to 25 years after becoming established. Prefers sandy soil; commonly found on river flood plains. During first stages of development of poplar stands, often mixed with willow and alder; white spruce often takes over after stands mature. Dies off in response to waterlogging.

behind tree roots or rocks or stuck firmly into mud surfaces. Large floating rafts of vegetation may also be assembled. Over a period of time, this material becomes waterlogged and sinks to the bottom, forming underwater food caches. Beavers may help this process along by dumping larger sections of peeled logs onto the mass, helping weigh it down.

Zoos that have beavers in their collections rarely rely on fresh trees to feed them. These captive animals are fed a variety of fresh vegetables and fruit, supplemented by dry rodent chow, but fresh tree limbs may also be added to the diet to provide gnawing material and keep their incisors from growing too long.

Beavers love corn, both sweet corn and field corn. They also raid fields for oats, wheat, clover, alfalfa, turnips, carrots, potatoes, rutabagas, and other vegetables. Orchards are also a favorite target because beavers are particularly fond of apples and like other fruit as well.

COMMUNICATION

*"Before diving, they strike the water with their tails,
& make such a noise that they can be heard more
than half a league away, & this is a warning to their
fellows, which causes them also to make a quick retreat."*

— Sieur de Dièreville (1708, *Relation of the Voyage
to Port Royal in Acadia or New France*)

Beavers are often thought of as quiet animals, their only sound generated by the slapping of their tails on the surface of the water. This is their standard alarm call and is frequently used, even when only a single beaver is around. Biologists have noted that female beavers, who are most often the leaders when it comes to dam and lodge construction, are responsible for making more of these alarm calls than males.

Not every tail slap is considered an alarm, however. Observers of beaver colonies note that although adult beavers perform this activity often, other beavers in the vicinity do not always respond by diving under the water, or if on land, rushing to the water's safety. They may be ignoring the signals because they recognize that a threat is not serious, or it may be a case of too many signals creating oversaturation.

When a threat remains in an area, beavers may remain alert and focused on the intruder, adding additional tail slaps every few minutes. And in some cases, the tail slap may be intended more for intimidation or warning than as an alarm call.

Beavers, however, are not mute. They can and do generate a wide variety of calls that are an important communication link in colonies. Baby beavers generate a high-pitched whine to solicit attention, cries that have been compared to that of human babies, puppies, or kittens. Adults also use a whining call, although this is descriptive of the sound and not an explanation of its use.

In the company of colony members, they also produce a mumbling low-pitched grunt, a soft "churring" sound, whimpers, shrill whines, whistles, grunts, and nasal-like noises. Chattering is sometimes also part of their verbal range and when confronted with danger, either a predator or intruding beaver from outside the colony, they generate an intense hissing threat call.

Some observers, standing outside occupied beaver lodges and listening to the beavers inside, have described the sound from within as a "rhythmic melody" or a "subdued concert."

Beavers also use some body language in their communications. The ears, although small, may indicate threat or fear if held down. The presence of intruders, including beavers from outside the colony, can trigger a special tooth-sharpening behavior, with the beaver gnashing its upper and lower incisors together as a threatening gesture. Although rare, beavers have been known to physically attack foreign beavers — with an occasional death resulting — and bites to humans and other animals are also on record.

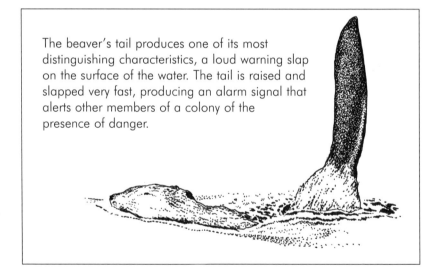

The beaver's tail produces one of its most distinguishing characteristics, a loud warning slap on the surface of the water. The tail is raised and slapped very fast, producing an alarm signal that alerts other members of a colony of the presence of danger.

PREDATORS

"It is a subject of regret that an animal so valuable and prolific should be hunted in a manner tending so evidently to the extermination of the species. ... A few individuals may, for a time, elude the immediate violence of persecution, and like the degraded descendants of the aboriginals of our soil, be occasionally exhibited as melancholy mementos of tribes long previously whelmed in the fathomless gulf of avarice."

— John Godman (1831, *American Natural History*)

Because of their large size, adult beavers face little danger from most predators. But they are ungainly and awkward on land, and their formidable front teeth are designed to chomp through trees, not attack other animals. At an early age, when young beavers are smaller and more vulnerable, they are preyed upon by a host of predators, both in and out of the water. These include coyotes, wolves, red foxes, martens, fishers, otters, mink, wolverines, bears, lynx, bobcats, mountain lions, and domestic dogs. Airborne threats come from larger raptors such as eagles, great horned owls, gray owls, red-tailed hawks, and goshawks.

Adult beavers are shy and quick to avoid danger but their only real threat comes from the largest predators such as wolves, black bears, grizzly bears, and wolverines. In urban areas, domestic dogs have also become a problem. In one study of an island ecosystem in Michigan where the only predator was timber wolves, beavers made up 11 percent of the wolves diet. In another study, beavers became more than half of the diet of wolves as the local population of deer declined from year to year.

In the southern part of their North American range, beavers may also find a threat from alligators, although younger individuals are more likely to be a target than adults. Large fish such as alligator gar and northern pike could also pose a threat.

BEAVER PREDATORS

MARTEN

RED-SHOULDERED HAWK

WOLVERINE

BLACK BEAR

GRAY WOLF

COYOTE

RED FOX

LOCOMOTION

"They begin to appear about Sundown, & must be approached very quietly, for it is most difficult to take them by surprise; their hearing is so acute that the slightest sound makes them dive at once, & when fear has driven them into the depths of the water, they are a long time in coming to the surface again, & always at a great distance from the place where they were alarmed."

— Sieur de Dièreville (1708, *Relation of the Voyage to Port Royal in Acadia or New France*)

Beavers are slow and awkward-looking on land. Although they are capable of short bursts of speed if necessary, their normal land gait is a rocking shuffle. In the water, on the other hand, the beaver's body shape and unique adaptations make it an efficient and graceful swimmer.

Because of its body fat and water-repellent fur, a beaver swims easily, although low in the water. During periods of the year when it is well fed and has a larger amount of fat under its skin, it is more buoyant. Native American hunters often avoided killing beavers in the spring or summer if they were in the water because the animals were leaner then and would sink to the bottom, making them hard to recover. Beaver kits, which begin swimming within weeks after their birth, are so buoyant that they float high in the water, bobbing like corks, and are unable to dive under the surface.

Beavers are strong, powerful swimmers. Using only their rear legs for propulsion, they can easily drag, carry, or push large limbs through the water, propelling themselves with paddling motions of their webbed rear feet. This webbing provides a surface area used to push against the water during the downward stroke; as the rear foot comes up after the downward stroke, the toes come together, constricting the webbing and reducing drag.

At slow speeds, propulsion comes only from paddling action pro-

99

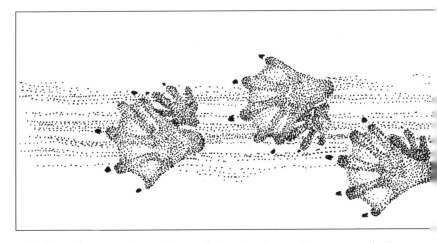

vided by the rear feet. Meanwhile, the front feet are tucked up against the chest, usually with the digits of the feet curled up in a ball. Most of the time, the tail remains extended to the rear, useful as a rudder but mostly inactive. When in a hurry underwater, however, beavers favor a different style, pumping their rear feet rapidly while undulating body and tail, adding to the force of propulsion.

In normal swimming activity both on the surface and submerged, beavers pump their rear feet together, but sometimes they may also use an alternating paddle. In long underwater swims, as when pursued or frightened, beavers in a hurry use a synchronized kick with both feet together, several kicks followed by a short glide without kicking.

Beavers usually swim at about two or three miles per hour during their daily activities in the water. They can maintain this speed on the surface or underwater. When startled, they can swim up to five or six miles per hour for short distances — either on the surface or underwater — and swim submerged for up to half a mile.

Swimming in dark or murky conditions, beavers may extend their front feet to protect themselves against collisions with unseen objects. When surfacing after a dive, they may also extend their front feet, probably to push away anything that is floating on the surface.

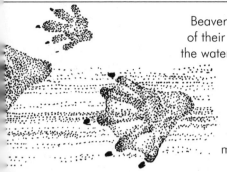

Beaver tracks on land are one indication of their relative awkwardness when out of the water. The tracks of the back feet often overlap that of the front, and the mark made by the tail, dragging along behind, often covers over these imprints. Often, the prints of a beaver's rear feet will be missing an imprint from the second inside toe, as this digit features a special double nail, used in grooming, that may not contact the ground.

On land, the beaver often drags its tail along the ground as it walks, but it can carry the tail slightly elevated. This posture is often used when it is carrying a branch or other material in its front legs or mouth, using the tail as an effective counterbalance. If startled or frightened while out of the water, a beaver can make short, clumsy dashes to the water, breaking into an uneven gallop.

Carrying branches, other vegetation, or mud, beavers use their front paws to hold the material against their bodies, the chin some-

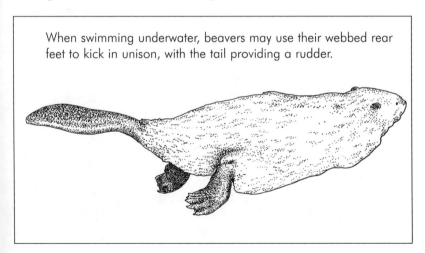

When swimming underwater, beavers may use their webbed rear feet to kick in unison, with the tail providing a rudder.

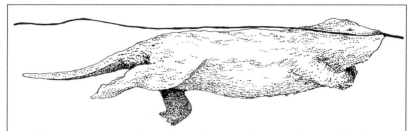

While swimming on the surface, beavers often use their webbed rear feet in an alternate paddling motion.

times pressed down to provide additional holding power. On land, they do this while in a semi-upright position, waddling along with their ungainly loads. They may also drag branches with only their mouths, all four feet in contact with the ground.

In the water, beavers also use their front legs to hold material. This causes them little problem because their propulsion in the water comes only from their rear feet. Beavers can swim on the surface carrying loads and have no problem doing the same underwater.

Beaver or muskrat? People often mistake muskrats for beavers when they are seen swimming on the surface of a body of water. Most of the time, it's a muskrat, because beavers are much more likely to be active only when people aren't around. Muskrats are also smaller than beavers and when swimming, display their long, thin tails, much different in shape than the tails of beavers.

FELLING SKILLS

"Before cutting a tree, a beaver usually paused and appeared to look at its surroundings as if choosing a place to squat or sit while cutting it down; but so far as I could tell, he gave no thought as to the direction in which the tree was going to fall."

— Enos A. Mills (1909, *Wild Life in the Rockies*)

Most of the abilities that beavers exhibit are instinctive capabilities governed by genetics. Young beavers do learn skills from their parents and are more accomplished as they gain experience, but the initial drive to cut down trees and build lodges and dams is born with them.

Beavers need to keep gnawing to wear down their ever-growing front teeth but the main reason they cut down trees is for food and construction material. During the initial periods when they are building lodges or dams, a colony may fell a dozen or more trees during a single night, but when selecting trees just for food, they average about a tree every other night.

Some observers have noted that when beavers fell trees, the trees always seem to fall toward the water, making them easier to drag away. But this useful skill is probably not a skill at all but the result of how trees grow. Trees that grow near water typically lean toward the water, influencing their fall in that direction, thanks to gravity.

Beavers sometimes drop trees in locations where they cannot be retrieved. They may also fell trees into thickets or other trees and abandon them without retrieval. Larger trees may temporarily attract their attention, but be abandoned before their gnawing has broken through the trunk. Not only are beavers capable of making these mistakes when felling trees, some are occasionally killed when the trees they are cutting fall on them.

A beaver begins its work on a selected tree by standing on its hind legs. This, the standard posture for a beaver at work, is an efficient position of strength because the animal uses its broad, flat tail like the third leg of a tripod. Turning its head to the side, the working cuts are made across the trunk and are spaced according to the diameter. If small in size — less than three to six inches in diameter — the beaver may cut directly through the stem with only a few bites, working from one side only.

Most of the time, however, it makes a series of two cuts, one high and one low, marking the width of its cutting target, and making cuts on more than one side before the tree falls. The larger the diameter of the tree, the wider apart the cuts.

With two cuts marking a cutting section, the beaver, still with its head turned to the side, anchors its upper incisors into the center of this section and uses its lower incisors to pry a chip of wood out of the trunk. Chips cut from beaver-felled trees are characterized by this action, sliced cleanly at the ends and splintered and shredded

To put its incisors to the most effective use, a beaver turns its head to the side, at right angles to the trunk of a tree, when cutting it down. Most of the cutting is the result of chunks of wood pried out with the action of its lower incisors.

in the middle. This action leaves a pattern of scoop-like marks in the wood, with the growing indentation forming an hourglass shape.

Trees with larger diameters require more cutting and more chips. As the cutting area works farther into the trunk, the chips often become smaller as the working area decreases. Observers have noted that when felling trees with harder wood, beavers create bigger chips than when working on softer woods such as aspen or willow.

The height at which trees are felled is relative to the size of the beaver doing the felling, with larger animals able to stand taller and cut higher. Beavers may also stand on downed trees, rocks, or overhanging banks to gain access to trees. And in the winter, snow can raise the working platform higher than in the summer, leaving trunks lopped off at heights that startle people when seen in the summer.

Usually, when chomping on larger trees, they are alert to the first sounds of weakness, the cracking and popping produced by breaking wood fibers. As a tree starts to fall, most beavers make a quick beeline for the closest water, diving in and under to get away.

When most trees are felled, the branches are gnawed off and retrieved, usually with the tree itself abandoned. Fallen trees with diameters of only a few inches are chewed into manageable

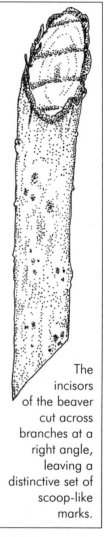

The incisors of the beaver cut across branches at a right angle, leaving a distinctive set of scoop-like marks.

sections, from a few feet to a few yards in length, and dragged away. Some of the time, beavers may remove and eat tree bark at the site where a tree is felled, but an instinctive fear of predators usually dictates that fallen material has to be food to go.

Although a single adult beaver typically works by itself while felling a tree, other family members and sometimes an entire colony will show up at a site after a tree is down, probably alerted by the sound of it falling. Communal dining is not uncommon and beavers rarely fight over food when dining together.

Large trees may take hours to fell and in some cases more than one night. Beavers are also known to work in pairs, with two or more adults trading off gnawing duty on the same tree trunk. But

Beavers are not known to climb trees, but they are able to reach up to their full height while standing on the ground in order to gain access to a tempting branch or to cut down a tree.

Almost every wood chip produced by a beaver while it is gnawing down a tree exhibits the characteristic marks of its incisors, a series of parallel grooves cutting across the grain. Because beavers select living trees for this activity, the chips are often light-colored and wet with sap when freshly cut. Within a few hours, the new chips will begin drying out and as this happens, the chips often curl or twist. Another common characteristic at many tree cutting sites is the uniform size of many of the chips.

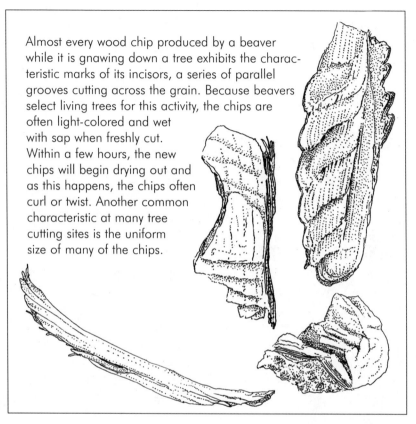

most of the time, the trees chosen for food are small enough to be felled in a matter of minutes. Soft woods such as willow or poplar in diameters of less than six inches can be chewed through in less than ten minutes.

The usual intent for branches and leaves from a downed tree is food. Large branches and trunks are used in construction, but branches and woody material of all sizes can also end up in dams and lodges. While the smaller branches can be carried in a beaver's mouth or dragged along the ground and through the water, bigger pieces require a different skill. Here, individual beavers and beavers working together move large pieces of timber by pushing them with

While swimming underwater, beavers are capable of carrying branches or heavy rocks, holding them against their chest and chin with their front paws.

their front paws, shoving them along with their noses and heads, or nudging them with their bodies. With this kind of force, logs are often rolled into the water rather than being pushed or pulled lengthwise.

In British Columbia, a beaver colony was known to cut down a large cottonwood tree that was 110 feet high. The diameter of the trunk was 67 inches, about 5½ feet thick. In other parts of North America, other large trees may be toppled, but these are exceptions to the typical beaver tree target.

Beavers don't always chew on wood just to cut it or eat it. They may select leftover sections of heavier branches and shred them with their teeth, creating a fluffy mass that is used to line bedding chambers.

Other than using their teeth to fell trees, beavers are also extremely handy with their front paws. These dextrous appendages are able to grasp limbs and rocks because of the flexible digits and a finger that works like the opposable thumb in humans. Beavers use their hands to gather rocks, mud, and woody debris, carrying it clutched under their chins or against their chests. In this posture, they are able to walk on their hind legs, leaning forward with their large tails providing a useful counterbalance.

In the water, they can manage a significant load of material with this method, using their webbed rear feet to provide propulsion. At the site of a lodge or dam, they use their hands to plaster mud against a mesh of branches and are able to manipulate branches, twisting and poking them into the framework.

The strong claws on their front paws are also used to dig dirt or mud. Beavers can be proficient diggers, evacuating long burrows and nesting chambers in the ground and scooping up masses of mud from the bottom of their ponds. In front of their dams, they often remove material to the depth of six to ten feet, using it for plastering the upstream side, at the same time increasing the water depth. When constructing canals, beavers also move large amounts of dirt and mud. Here, the mud is usually deposited along the sides of the excavations.

BEAVER DAMS

"The influence of a beaver-dam is astounding. As soon as completed, it becomes a highway for the folk of the wild. It is used day and night. ... Over it dash pursuer and pursued; and on it take place battles and courtships. It is often torn by hoof and claw of animals locked in death-struggles, and often, very often, it is stained with blood. Many a drama, picturesque, fierce, and wild, is staged upon a beaver-dam."

— Enos A. Mills (1909, *Wild Life on the Rockies*)

Beavers are driven by necessity to build dams. Dams increase the depth of water, thereby protecting them from predators. Except for the quest for food, this is their number one priority. But if there is already enough water at a site, as in many rivers and lakes, beavers live comfortably without this kind of construction.

Dam sites may be narrow, shallow regions of running water, but beavers also construct dams in other types of terrain. Wherever they begin building, gathering materials and construction is always done from the upstream side. And often, no matter what the site, the beavers doing the building take full advantage of any tree roots, rocks, or other protrusions in the water. These provide effective anchors against which to pile and prop branches, also from the upstream side.

Observers have long noted that some beaver dams, especially large ones, seem to have an upstream "bow," curving into the flow of water and thereby increasing the strength of the structures, just as in those built by human engineers. This is not a careful engineering feat on the part of the beavers, however, but the result of water current on the beavers' dam-building activity. When dams are built from the banks out, the current interferes with new material as it is brought to the site, dragging it into the material already in place. The faster the current — and it is usually faster in the mid-

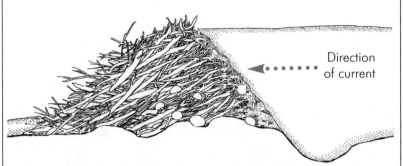

CROSS-SECTION OF A BEAVER DAM

Direction of current

Beaver dams may look like disorganized piles of branches and logs, but they are usually tightly jammed together, with most of the wood placed parallel to the flow of water. On the upstream side, the side facing the pond, the surface of the dam is often packed with mud, small rocks, and other organic material, forming a dense barrier that holds the water back.

dle of a stream — the quicker it pushes material together. When beavers begin building from a mid-stream island or rock, bowing is much less likely to happen.

As a beaver brings branches to a dam site, the water current exerts the greatest drag on the leafy sections, orienting a branch so that the butt ends face upstream. In the initial stages of dam construction, most of the branches used point upstream.

Branches in dams are typically jammed together creating an interwoven mass, an instinctive practice that gives the structure much of its strength. In many dam sites, some branches or gnawed-off sections of tree trunk are pushed end-first into the muddy bottom, creating anchor points for subsequent material. Even if there are natural obstructions such as protruding rocks and tree roots, beavers will dig up, push, and carry rocks to the site to help anchor the branches they have begun to amass. Large adult beavers are capable of moving stones weighing up to thirty or forty pounds, pushed and rolled into place.

Trees selected for dam building may be the same as those used for feeding, but not always. Conifers, including pine, cedar, and spruce trees, are not often selected as food but are cut for use in dams and lodges. In some dam sites, biologists have noted that the animals seem to prefer trees of a similar size, with most of the branches used of a similar diameter.

As the water flow begins to slow, the beavers will begin adding other materials to the dam structure. These are mostly mud, rocks, and chunks of sod scooped from banks or stream bottoms with their front legs and carried to the site. The debris is plastered in with the branches, creating strong, bonded sections. Cornstalks taken from nearby gardens and fields have also been noted in some dams.

Much of this caulking material comes from the section directly upstream of the dam site. As the mud and rocks are dug out, the pond depth is increased. Dam caulking is done from the upstream side, creating a solid mass against which the water pushes. Unlike the downstream side, which is typically a loose, ragged jumble of protruding limbs, the upstream side is more vertical and often smoother, the result of the relentless effort beavers make to stop the flow of water.

After the major flow of water ceases, beavers respond to the sound of water "leaks," or currents trickling and cascading through holes, breaks, and low spots. This sound produces an instinctive reaction, drawing them directly to the spot where water is escaping. Gathering mud and rocks, they will dump and pack material into a hole until the sound of rushing water subsides.

The dam-building sequence is directly related to the level of water. Beavers do not build in sections, but in layers. As the water rises, they add material uniformly across the top, raising the structure a little at a time until a desired level of water has been impounded.

In many locations, this kind of damming construction forces a pool of water to spread out into the surrounding area and around the ends of the dam itself. Beavers will respond to this water movement by adding extensions and additional dams until the water

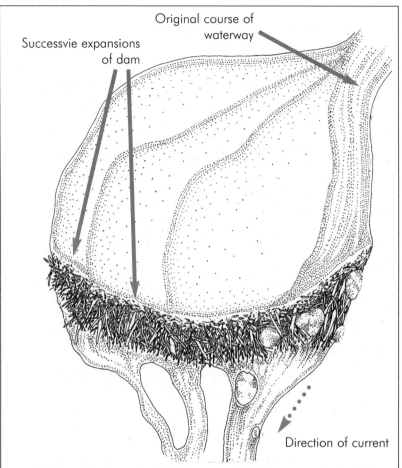

Successvie expansions of dam

Original course of waterway

Direction of current

As the dam begins to hold back water, the rising stream behind the dam often floods out into the surrounding terrain, requiring beavers to expand the original structure.

movement ceases to trigger their response. Many beaver dams constructed like this turn out to be long chains, twisting and changing direction as dictated by natural obstacles and the terrain.

When a beaver dam is constructed well, it can be surprisingly effective at holding in water. Over time, seeds may sprout and the fresh limbs used in its construction may root, adding strength and permanence to the structure. But despite this effectiveness, the average beaver dam looks more like a messy pile of branches than a carefully-planned fabrication.

Although the normal activity of beavers is building and repairing dams, they have also been observed altering their work to lower water levels. Probably due to flood conditions that raise the water level inside lodges, the crown of a dam may be reduced in one or more places to allow a flow of water out of the beaver's reservoir. In some stream sites, beavers may also channel excess water through wider, heavier sections of their dams to reduce the scouring effects of the water on the structures.

Some reports also claim that beavers deliberately lower the level of the water in their ponds during the winter months when ice forms solidly on the top. By doing this, they create an air space between the ice and the water, giving them practical use of the water when access to the land is cut off by the ice. However, this kind of water control is probably not because of active engineering on the part of the beavers. Rather, it comes from a natural decrease in water flow that occurs in winter months in cold climates.

Beaver dams are as much the result of perseverance as skill. Many, if not most, attempts at dam building result in breaks or complete failure. The largest dams are not the work of beavers with greater skills, but the work of more beavers over longer periods of time. Although an average beaver dam may only be in use for ten years or less, some have been in place for much longer and are the result of continuing work by generations of animals.

Dams on small streams can be built from scratch in a span of several nights. During an average season, however, the urge to dam may trigger more dam-building activity than is actually needed to create an adequate pond. Beavers are also known to add branches, mud, and other typical dam-building material to already existing man-made dams, apparently driven by instinct alone.

In most parts of North America, beaver dams are no more than two to three feet high and span from 50 to 100 feet of water. The

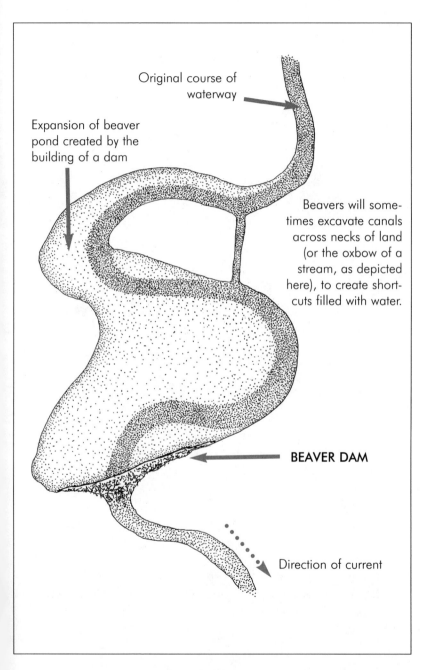

Original course of waterway

Expansion of beaver pond created by the building of a dam

Beavers will sometimes excavate canals across necks of land (or the oxbow of a stream, as depicted here), to create shortcuts filled with water.

BEAVER DAM

Direction of current

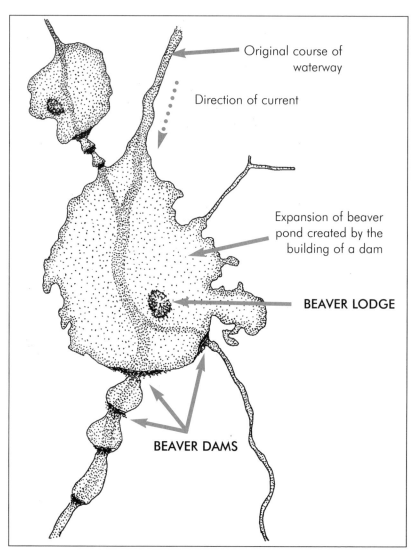

Original course of
waterway

Direction of current

Expansion of beaver
pond created by the
building of a dam

BEAVER LODGE

BEAVER DAMS

largest known dams have been up to ten feet high and a few have spanned up to 500 feet. At one site on the Jefferson River in Montana, a beaver dam was measured at more than 2,100 feet long.

Larger dams are often strong enough to support the weight of an

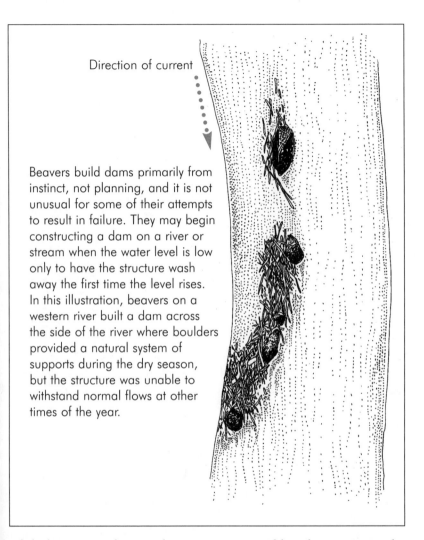

Direction of current

Beavers build dams primarily from instinct, not planning, and it is not unusual for some of their attempts to result in failure. They may begin constructing a dam on a river or stream when the water level is low only to have the structure wash away the first time the level rises. In this illustration, beavers on a western river built a dam across the side of the river where boulders provided a natural system of supports during the dry season, but the structure was unable to withstand normal flows at other times of the year.

adult human and some have proven capable of supporting the weight of a horse and rider. Smaller dams may only be one or two feet wide along the top; the larger ones can be up to five or six feet across.

Some large beaver ponds have secondary dams at sites downstream from the main dams. Some observers have speculated that these smaller units are the result of the beavers' advanced engineering skills, built to raise the level of water downstream from large dams, thereby evening the water pressure on the dam and reducing the risk of a blowout. But a more likely explanation is that when large ponds are created, they signify healthy colonies and ample supplies of food. These conditions help trigger faster population growth in a colony, producing more animals available to do more dam building. And beavers typically build additional dams in the vicinity of the original structure to increase the areas available for safe swimming.

Beavers not only build dams to create bodies of water, they are known to construct canals. These waterways are used as safe passages to extended foraging areas. Because beavers are clumsy and vulnerable on land, canals provide an effective alternate route. These canals can be three feet wide or wider and three feet deep or deeper, which is ample room for beavers to swim while carrying food, but they are often no more than a foot or two in depth and extend out from the edges of a pond into the tree-laden land.

Beaver canals are found more often in western parts of North America than in the east and are more likely to be constructed where the terrain is relatively flat. Some canals have been noted on lakes and ponds where the land may protrude out into the water in one or more spots. Here, beavers may dig "shortcuts" through the obstructing land in order to shorten the distance they have to swim. In streams where there are naturally occurring meanders, or oxbows, beaver canals have also been used to create shortcuts.

The large, strong claws on the front feet are used as digging implements during canal building. Using the same techniques, beavers sometimes create extra depth in ponds by digging "underwater canals." These are used as thoroughfares to link lodges with submerged caches of food. The trenches also help prove safe passage during periods of low water.

Just as canals serve as effective passageways with water, beavers create regular trails on land. They do not deliberately construct these trails, however, but generate them from repeated use of the

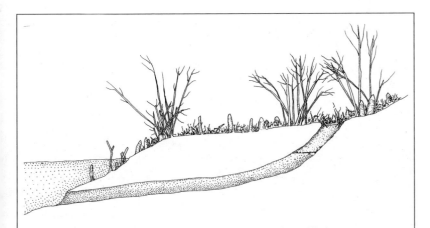

Along with canals on the surface, beavers also will dig escape tunnels leading to feeding areas away from the water. These systems, known as "plunge holes," help expand their effective feeding area without exposing them to additional risk from predators.

same routes to and from supplies of food. Near the water, these beaver trails may be muddy slides, helping facilitate entry into the water.

There are also examples of beavers using tunnels to extend their safety zone away from the water. Tunnels can run for dozens of feet into the surrounding grazing areas, ending in openings called "plunge holes." Plunge holes provide a quick and effective escape hatch to enter the water's safety without having to be exposed for any great distance on the surface of the ground.

BEAVER LODGES

"As for me, I know well that there are many men, even skilled in many things, who would be greatly embarrassed if it were necessary for them to build their dwellings for themselves, especially if they had to take so many and important precautions for the preservation of their life as the Beavers must take in regard to their breathing, their food, the water, and the care to conceal themselves from the knowledge of the hunters."

— Nicolas Denys (1672, *The Description and Natural History of the Coasts of North America*)

Throughout their North American range, beavers live in both lodges and burrows. The appropriate choice of a lodge or a burrow is partially dependent on the amount and constancy of the water supply; in deep, fast-moving streams and rivers, lodges are not practical or needed. In Europe, more beavers live in burrows than lodges. A longer history of being hunted by humans possibly influenced this less conspicuous choice.

Lodge building may begin before, during, or after the construction of a dam. Some biologists believe that when young adult beavers first migrate away from home, typically after they are two years old, the first thing they do after finding a mate is to dig a burrow. They use this burrow as their main den until after their first winter, when they begin building either a dam or a lodge. Beavers that live in burrows are sometimes called "bank beavers" because the burrows are on the banks of streams or lakes.

Some observers also note that lodge-building activity is more common in the late summer and early fall, when the shortened hours of daylight trigger an instinct for shelter. The lodge represents an improved chance of survival in winter conditions. But even with the strong instinct for survival that drives the lodge-building, beavers do not always succeed in making a habitable structure.

Younger beavers may put together flimsy lodges that fall apart or wash away and beavers often have lodges destroyed by rising water or floods. The strongest lodges, however, are often capable of surviving floods, with the inhabitants temporarily displaced until the water level recedes.

A lodge site may be on marshy ground that is filling with water or under the level of water already accumulated. More often than not, lodge sites are on the northern side of ponds, probably placed to take advantage of extra sunlight. Sometimes, beavers will find a high point or rise on which to begin their construction, making subsequent work easier. On this spot, they carry mud, stones, and other debris in their front paws, dumping it to create a raised bed or island. As the water rises, more material is added, gradually producing a floor that is elevated above the surface of the water. The lodge base can be built using less mud and more branches, or with branches only.

Branches, tree limbs, leaves, sod, and other leafy materials are piled up on this platform, forming a ragged, rounded mound. But there is less simple piling and more determined jamming and inter-

A typical beaver lodge looks like a large, messy pile of logs, branches, and leaves, sometimes partially covered with a layer of mud. Although muskrat lodges may sometimes be almost as large as a beaver lodge, the muskrats build theirs of reeds and other softer plant material, with little or no wood involved.

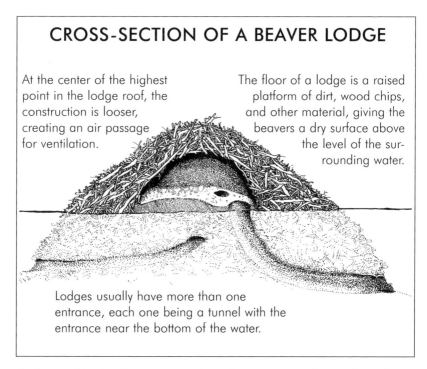

CROSS-SECTION OF A BEAVER LODGE

At the center of the highest point in the lodge roof, the construction is looser, creating an air passage for ventilation.

The floor of a lodge is a raised platform of dirt, wood chips, and other material, giving the beavers a dry surface above the level of the surrounding water.

Lodges usually have more than one entrance, each one being a tunnel with the entrance near the bottom of the water.

locking of limbs. Beavers use their front paws and mouth to shove sticks into this growing mass, pushing them in as far as possible. With longer branches, they sometimes push them in, then lop them off with their teeth. The remaining length is then jammed in also.

When the mound is sufficiently large, they hollow out a clearing in the mass to create a nesting chamber. This clearing is achieved with the same tool that the beaver uses to obtain its woody building material — by using its teeth. The chips and shredded particles that are by-products of this interior work help create an insulating layer on the floor.

A typical beaver lodge has a single interior room of six to eight feet in diameter and two to three feet in height at the center. As a room is created, the walls of the lodge are strengthened with the addition of rocks, mud, sod, leaves, and more branches, until they are about two or three feet thick.

One or more air holes at the top provides ventilation, but this is more an accident of construction than a planned feature. As beavers pile up materials to form the top of a lodge, they spend less time packing and condensing it, creating a looser framework that creates a natural conduit for fresh air. In cold weather, lodges that are occupied indicate the presence of inhabitants by the clouds of condensation rising from the ventilation holes.

At least one entryway is constructed in each lodge. This opens directly into the water and is wide enough for an adult beaver to swim easily in or out. In a large lodge, the main entry is lined with

INSIDE SCHEMATIC OF A BEAVER LODGE

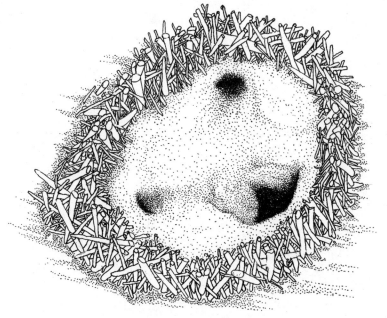

Some beavers dig three, four, or even more entrances to their lodges. Some of these underwater tunnels are only big enough for an adult beaver to swim through; others are much larger in diameter in order to make room for beavers carrying branches for food.

mud, allowing quick slides into the water. Often, one or more additional entrances are included, sometimes adapted to allow more room for beavers carrying food into the lodge. In a lodge with multiple entryways, there is often a clear difference in size, indicating which is used for dragging in branches and which is meant just for the beavers alone.

The coming of cold weather, foreshadowed by the shortening hours of daylight, triggers additional lodge construction activity for beavers, especially in the northern parts of their range. To lodges built in previous years, they add mud, organic debris, and other loose matter to the exposed walls. When it gets below freezing, this moist material solidifies, adding a dense, hard barrier to potential intruders. Mud plastering can also be a continual activity through the year, as erosion from rainfall and flooding is a constant threat.

Some large beaver lodges have been used continuously for gener-

When beavers live on deep lakes or fast-moving rivers, they may not construct lodges out in the water, but use burrows or lodges built directly on the banks. Depending on water depth near the shore, these structures may include fortified underwater tunnels that lead to deeper water.

CROSS-SECTION OF A BANK BURROW

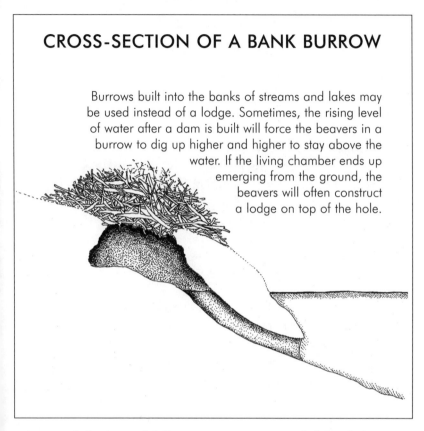

Burrows built into the banks of streams and lakes may be used instead of a lodge. Sometimes, the rising level of water after a dam is built will force the beavers in a burrow to dig up higher and higher to stay above the water. If the living chamber ends up emerging from the ground, the beavers will often construct a lodge on top of the hole.

ations, with beavers of different ages in an extended family living in the same dwelling. Lodges have been found with more than one chamber, but multiple chambers are not the norm. Where more than one chamber exists, each chamber has at least one entrance burrow.

Beavers also frequently "remodel" their lodges as their family size increases, the water level rises, or the lodge itself settles into a more compact mass. As always, they use their teeth to cut out extra space from the sides or above, as needed. The material that is removed drops to the floor, raising it.

From the outside, typical beaver lodges rise five to eight feet out of the water and appear to be rough jumbles of branches and other organic material, conical or rounded in shape. The exteriors may be from 20 to 40 feet in diameter. In the far northern extremes of their range, beavers that live in habitats with few or no trees may construct lodges without branches, using roots and stalks of whatever vegetation is handy. Rocks and mud help keep such materials cemented together.

Sometimes beavers construct lodges from what were originally burrows. In these circumstances, the bank tunnels are extended upward as water levels rise. If the top of the burrow gets too close to the surface or breaks through, the beavers will begin piling mud, branches, and other building materials over the top. In some cases, the burrow will then extend out of the ground and start to resemble a traditional lodge structure.

In parts of their range, beavers build and use both lodges and burrows. But in some areas, rocky ground or permafrost may prevent the digging of burrows, limiting them to lodges. In other areas, only burrows are built. This use of burrows is primarily linked to habitat, with deep, constantly-running rivers eliminating the need for lodges. Large rivers such as the Mississippi, Missouri, and the Ohio all have beaver colonies along some stretches using burrows for their dens. The same is true for some larger lakes.

Burrows that are used as primary lodging may begin as nothing more than upwardly sloping tunnels that start under the surface of the water and extend up and into a dirt bank. Near the surface of the water but inside the burrow, a widened area is dug out to use as a feeding chamber. A nesting chamber is typically farther up in the tunnel and lined with dry grasses, leaves, and wood chips.

As with lodges, most burrows have more than one entrance. Burrows can extend at right angles from the water into a bank or diverge and run parallel to the water. Beaver burrows are wide enough to permit easy passage for the adults, usually two or three feet in diameter, and are sometimes large enough for an adult human to crawl through. In some cases, these burrows can extend for up to 100 feet, although most are not this long.

Throughout their range, beaver colonies are often on the move. They remain in one area for a few years or more if there is ample food available, but sooner or later, they reduce the supply of trees and head to new areas. The burrows and lodges they leave behind are not wasted, however. Muskrats, raccoons, otters, and other mammals use these constuctions for their own dens. The exterior walls of lodges are also sometimes employed as a base for bird nests. In some cases, smaller mammals such as muskrats may inhabit a beaver lodge while beavers are still using it.

TERRITORY

*"The social habits of the beaver are shown also by
the fact that several families, if I may use the term,
will occupy one and the same dwelling ... More
wonderful still, if they become so crowded as to
inconvenience one another, part of them will withdraw
voluntarily, take their belongings with them, and look for
new abodes along the banks of the streams."*

— Father François du Creux
(1664, *History of Canada or New France*)

Although beavers are communal animals, living in colonies of a
few or more animals, they are not very tolerant of other
colonies. Competition for food resources is a critical factor in their
survival, generating a strong sense of territory.

Most of the time they mark and maintain this territory without
aggression, relying on the specialized scent organs called castor
glands. The pungent fluid from these glands is used to constantly
replenish marking sites that are located along the edges of their
waterways, either lakes or streams.

The scenting sites — called castor piles, castor paddies, musk
bogs, or sign heaps — are low mounds of mud or organic debris,
scraped and piled together near or at the water line. Usually no
more than one or two feet high, several of these piles may be found
in the territory of each colony. All the adult beavers, both males and
females, make regular visits to the mounds to deposit fresh scent,
often on a daily basis. The scent is deposited from the castor glands
— located close to their anal vents — directly onto the top of the
mounds and sometimes fresh mud or litter is added. Urination is also
part of the process.

The scent is a powerful signal to other beavers and colonies as
beavers are able to detect the scent of foreign beavers from some distance away. Fur trappers have long taken advantage of this beaver
characteristic in their hunting methods. They cut out the castor

glands from a slain beaver and save the contents, using it to bait traps.

Beavers have an innate sense regarding the food-carrying capacity of their territory. When food supplies are scarce, entire colonies will migrate to new locations. There are also indications that the size of litters and even the number of pregnancies of female beavers may be directly related to the food available in an area. As new generations are born, young adult beavers move out of the colony, usually in the second or third year, and seek their own territory, leaving the original territory with a more or less constant balance of food and animals.

Although beavers generally live in colonies, individual beavers are often found living alone. Both female and male beavers who are solitary are called "bachelors." This may be a temporary or permanent condition depending on the availability of suitable mates. Even though adult beavers are generally monogamous and will typically

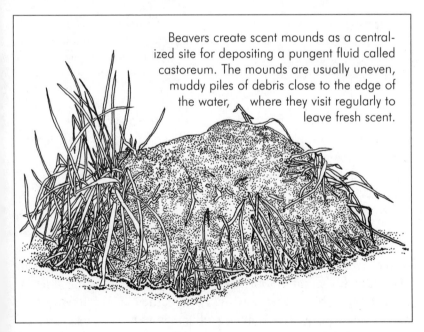

Beavers create scent mounds as a centralized site for depositing a pungent fluid called castoreum. The mounds are usually uneven, muddy piles of debris close to the edge of the water, where they visit regularly to leave fresh scent.

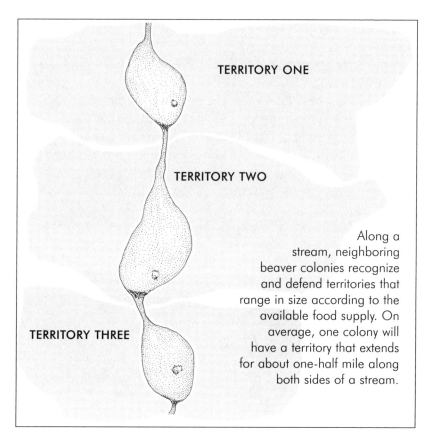

TERRITORY ONE

TERRITORY TWO

TERRITORY THREE

Along a stream, neighboring beaver colonies recognize and defend territories that range in size according to the available food supply. On average, one colony will have a territory that extends for about one-half mile along both sides of a stream.

stay with one mate for a lifetime, the death of a mate can trigger a male or a female to seek out another partner.

In a single colony, two parents might live with more than one generation of offspring. The young from the current season can be joined by the adolescents from the previous year and in some cases, even those that were born two years previously. All participate in activities such as lodge and dam building and repair, and also bring food to feed the young. The average size of beaver colonies is about five individuals, but colonies with more than ten are not uncommon. Although colonies usually live together in one lodge, some lodges might have more than one chamber and in some beaver territories, more than one lodge is used simultaneously.

Various studies have measured the number of beavers that live in a given amount of territory. This density ranges from one to two colonies per square mile (0.38 to 0.76 colonies per square km). Another useful measurement is the ratio of colonies to length of stream, as all beaver territories are centered around water. Studies have found ratios of .06 to 1.2 colonies per mile of waterway (0.1 to 1.9 colonies per km).

In North America, the population density is generally related to latitude. In the north, the density of colonies is lower and in the south it's higher, mostly due to the seasonal availability of food.

When colonies move to new territories, or young beavers set out to establish their own territory, beavers usually move only a few miles. In one study, the average distance of migration was 4.6 miles, with an upper range of ten to thirty miles. Beavers can move much farther, however, with records showing some displaced animals ending up 150 miles from their starting point. When young adult beavers leave colonies located on streams or rivers, they usually head downstream. Because the prime habitat for beavers is usually located at the headwaters or upstream portions of waterways, these areas are usually claimed first and migrating beavers that head upstream are less likely to find open, unclaimed territory.

Although calamities such as forest fires or flooding might force relocation at any time of the year, most beaver movement happens in the spring. The end of icing conditions on waterways is a major trigger for movement, as is the development of new growth in trees and local vegetation.

Fire may have been one of the greatest traditional factors in the development of beaver ranges in the north. Fire among evergreen forests tends to clear away large stands of trees, creating conditions ripe for the rapid growth of aspen and birch, among other species. As beavers greatly prefer these fast-growing trees to conifers, fire may be an important first step in producing prime beaver territory.

Currently, in national parks and forests in North America, where modern management has focused on reducing the damage from forest fires, some scientists believe that the original balance of beaver colonies and their prime habitat may have been negatively affected. Without fire, forests tend to favor the slower growing conifers, reducing the number and acreage of clearings where aspen, willow, and birch find the best growing conditions.

Natural cycles of migration also involve beavers moving away from territory as it is "eaten out," leaving too little vegetation to sustain them. But as they move into nearby territory that has fresh supplies of their favored trees, the original territory is left behind to recover. Within a few years, the colony might return, repairing and reusing their original lodges and dams.

THE ECOLOGY OF BEAVER PONDS

"In midsummer, near most beaver homes one finds columbines, fringed blue gentians, orchids, and lupines blooming, while many of the ponds are green and yellow with pond-lilies."

— Enos A. Mills (1909, *Wild Life in the Rockies*)

Beavers are an important force for change in most of the habitats in which they reside. Particularly because of the standing water that is impounded by their dams, the frequency and diversity of other life forms is affected. And this change continues after beavers leave an area and abandon their dams. Much of the terrain in the watersheds of their range includes meadows and open areas created from the build-up of silt and sediment while the dams were active.

In regions where there are healthy populations of beavers, up to 40 percent of the streams and rivers in the headwaters of a watershed can be affected by their building activity. In the terrain surrounding beaver ponds, an estimated 15 percent of the foliage may also be impacted by waterlogging, tree felling, and other foraging by these animals.

As a dam is built on a running stream, the water behind it slows and builds into a pool. Even though some water always continues flowing or seeping through a dam when it is completed, the effect is to create a deeper aquatic habitat than existed before, raising the temperature of the water and decreasing the oxygen content.

Not only is the visible water level raised, but the level of the local water table as well. This elevation can have a positive effect on some kinds of vegetation — those with shallow root systems that thrive in wet conditions, and a negative effects on others — trees that are adapted to dry ground conditions, for example. In some parts of the country, this kind of local rise in the water table can reverse the damage from regional droughts.

For some fish, such as a few species of trout, the pond may be less desirable than the running water that was there before; other species find the pool conditions an advantage. Part of this preference is because of the physical requirements of each species — some fish are adapted to live in colder water, some require higher oxygen content — and part comes from the change in food sources. Just as the fish find certain water conditions better than others, so too do plankton, algae, insects, and other life forms that provide food for the fish.

The physical presence of a beaver dam on a stream is also a specific factor in changing the ecosystem of a free-flowing stream. When the dam is in place, it forms a block that stops most forms of life from moving upstream, especially fish. This can cause temporary or permanent concentrations of fish at the downstream side of a beaver dam site.

As beaver ponds are first formed, an initial rush of new animal life may occur. Birds in particular may spot a pond first and gravitate to the resting and feeding opportunities it provides. Waterfowl, migrating species, raptors, and songbirds respond to the creation of a new pond. Most beaver ponds have a larger population of birds and a greater number of bird species in and around them than found in the terrain before the ponds were created. Among the waterfowl that are thought to have a critical link to beaver ponds for breeding and brood rearing are the mallard, the wood duck, the black duck, mergansers, the ring-necked duck, and the green- and blue-winged teal. Individual birds and bird species may favor beaver ponds because unlike many kinds of free-standing bodies of water, the water level is maintained at a more or less even depth, improving the chances that nest sites for waterfowl will be protected throughout a breeding season.

The variety of insect species typically found in a free-flowing stream will change after a beaver dam is built. The temperature and oxygen content of the water — both behind the dam and downstream from it — are altered by the blockage of water, making the local aquatic ecosystem less supportive for many of the insects that

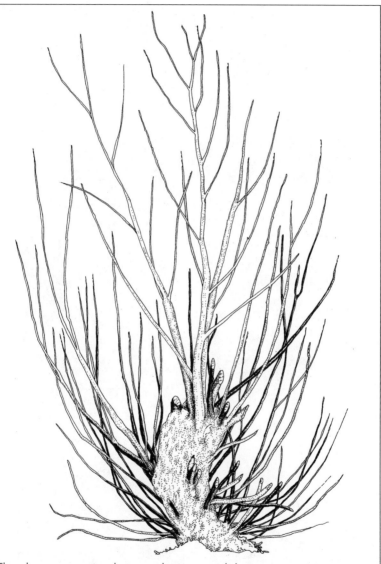

The close connection between beavers and their environment is exemplified by some of the trees they favor as food. In trees such as this willow, cutting by beavers triggers the growth of new branches, providing fresh foliage and food for the beaver.

ANIMAL DIVERSITY

Some species of songbirds, waterfowl, and raptors may be attracted to a beaver pond ecosystem as a permanent base. Other species take advantage of the open water and sources of food as a stop-over during migration.

The water source nourishes many types of flowering plants that attract insects in abundance.

Aquatic insects that thrive in cold running water may find the warmer, slow-flowing water of the pond less than ideal, but other species thrive in these conditions.

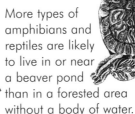

More types of amphibians and reptiles are likely to live in or near a beaver pond than in a forested area without a body of water.

Trees killed by the rising waters of the pond and the rich sediment that builds up on the bottom attract a wide variety of insects and other life forms.

Beaver ponds provide a well-balanced environment for many kinds of fish, especially those which feed on the forms of insect life that thrive in these kinds of bodies of water.

PLANT DIVERSITY

Many of the trees that form a major part of the beavers' diet thrive in the moist soil found near streams and ponds. Some existing trees may die as the water level in a pond begins to rise and covers their roots, but others thrive in the open, unshaded ground cleared by the beavers.

Plants such as reeds and sedges that thrive in marshy conditions benefit from the expanding wetlands created by beaver ponds.

Algae and other water plants that may be missing or sparse in fast-flowing streams grow quickly in the warmer water behind a beaver dam. These plants provide a significant secondary source of food to the beavers.

Water that is backed up by a beaver dam can have a big impact on the water table, raising it by several feet or more. The higher water table not only nourishes the root systems of the plants above, it creates a hidden reservoir of water that can provide significant life support during warm weather and drought conditions.

were already there. But at the same time, species of aquatic insects that thrive in the new conditions take over. Frogs, salamanders, and other semi-aquatic animal forms also quickly expand in number and diversity after a pond forms.

In some regions, beaver ponds may be the most common type of impounded water and create critical habitats for some species that do not flourish when there is only running water. As beaver ponds mature, reptiles increase in number and the diversity of reptile species multiplies. In studies of beaver ponds in headwater areas, the diversity of fish species increased to a maximum level when a pond was between nine and seventeen years old, and then declined.

The standing water, with its higher temperature and altered oxygen content, becomes a prime breeding ground for many plants that are less likely to be found in running water, if at all. But this diversity comes with a price. As the water backs up and spreads out behind a dam, it often covers the roots and lower trunks of trees in the area, those that have not been targeted as food or building material by the beavers.

For most of these trees, the sudden change in environment is catastrophic and the result is death. Although this represents a loss of trees, the resulting dead wood attracts even more wildlife — insects that target dying trees and animals that seek out these insects for food. Dead trees can also provide an important source of nest sites for birds and some small mammals.

Vegetation that flourishes in the impounded water is often a critical part of the diet of beavers. The dams they build are a safety device, creating water barriers between them and predators, but they also produce ongoing harvests of water lilies, reeds, mosses, and other water plants. In some parts of their range and during some seasons, beavers often eat more of this kind of vegetation than they do trees.

In some parts of North America, the normal cycle of beaver foraging may not work to their advantage. As they cut down the trees closest to their water supply, the wet, marshy conditions created by their ponds can help new trees to sprout. But these same conditions are ideal grazing conditions for elk, animals which prefer the tender young vegetation provided by sprouting trees.

The elk that are attracted to the mature beaver ponds can then out-graze the beavers, depriving them of easily available food. The only solution for the beavers is to move away in search of new territory, leaving their former habitat to the elk and other grazers.

The dam also affects another quality of the water supply. Slowed and stopped in its downslope run, the sediment carried along in a beaver stream drops and settles to the bottom. Depending on the amount of sediment naturally occurring in a stream, the result of a dam can be a slow or a rapid build-up of material suspended in the water. Beavers generally deal with some of this material in their normal construction activity, digging it up and using it to add plastering to their dams and lodges. This not only adds strength to these structures, it maintains the depth of water they need.

Not only is the amount of sediment in the water of a stream decreased by the presence of a beaver dam, the water behind the dam can have lower levels of phosphorus and nitrogen. Studies of beaver ponds in the West also show an increase in the pH value of the water. Water downstream from a beaver dam usually has less oxygen than in similar streams without such constructions.

Breaks sometime occur in the dams, the result of sudden rises in water depth or seasonal flooding. When a dam breaks, at least one result may benefit the resident beavers. The sudden increase in water flow can scour out sediment that has built up in the beaver pond, increasing the depth of water when the dam is rebuilt and adding more life to the beaver's territory. But sudden breaks in beaver dams can also have a negative domino effect downstream, because the initial rush of water is stronger and heavier than that produced by local conditions. As this surge travels downstream, it can cause severe damage, including knocking out other beaver lodges and dams.

BEAVER DISEASES

"The beaver is an amphibious quadruped which cannot live for any long time in the water, and it is said is even able to exist entirely without it, provided it has the convenience of sometimes bathing itself."

—Jonathan Carver, (1788, *Travels Through the Interior Parts of North America*)

Mammals that live in colonies often suffer from chronic health problems. Beavers are no exception. Along with fleas, beaver families pass along beetles that live in their fur, sucking blood for food. Other parasites include lice, mites, ticks, roundworms, flies, flukes, nematodes, screwworms, ringworms, trematodes, and a variety of harmful protozoa.

Infectious organisms in the water include giardia, which is spread through feces to animals throughout a watershed, including humans. Giardia, now widespread throughout the western states, was once found mainly in beaver habitat, inspiring the name "beaver fever."

The biggest threat to beavers is tularemia. This disease is spread through the water and is caused by a bacterium called *Francisella tularensis*. Extremely contagious to beavers, this disease often spreads through multiple colonies, causing hundreds or thousands of deaths. Also called "rabbit fever," it can also be spread through insect bites and has been known to infect and kill large numbers of beavers during some outbreaks. Humans can contract this disease, but it is rarely fatal. Beavers are also susceptible to rabies, lung fungus, distemper, a form of tuberculosis, and lumpy jaw.

Starvation is a constant threat to beavers at higher altitudes and in northern parts of their range. Although they are instinctively driven to migrate to new areas when food supplies dwindle, extreme cold weather or excessive snowfall can trap them. Beavers are also injured and killed by falling trees, the victims of their own felling

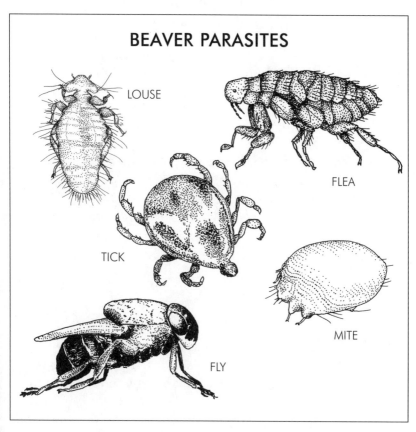

BEAVER PARASITES

LOUSE

FLEA

TICK

MITE

FLY

activity. More often, they are trapped and drowned in lodges or burrows during floods or sudden increases in water depth.

Despite the threat from predators and disease, most beaver deaths are caused by humans, including trapping and accidents resulting from beavers living too near roadways. As beavers gradually repopulate more of their traditional range, they are also more likely to encounter human developments, where domestic dogs can be a menace, attacking and killing both young and adult animals.

THE GREAT
BEAVER TRADE

*"Wasteful and unnecessary as was the destruction of
the wild buffalo herds on the upper Missouri and country
tributary thereto by the hide hunters and wolfers, the
destruction of the beaver along water courses of the same
range was fully as inexcusable besides being positively
detrimental to the water courses themselves by the
destruction through neglect and disuse of the great chain
of reservoirs established by the beaver and used so
beneficially in the life of these long and narrow streams
that wind their separate way across the face of the great
treeless plains."*

— A. Radclyffe Dugmore (1914, *The Romance of the Beaver*)

In parts of Canada as well as the western territories of the United States, much of the trade in beaver skins involved native tribes. Rather than do the trapping themselves, early settlers were more likely to be traders, exchanging goods with tribes for beaver pelts. These goods, in great demand among the Native Americans, included tobacco, beads, mirrors, axes, cloth such as calico, blankets, rifles, lead and gunpowder, and alcohol.

In Canada in the 1600s, Samuel de Champlain initiated an informal system based on "coureurs de bois," French explorers who accompanied Indian hunters and helped encourage the trading of fur for tools, weapons, and other commodities. After a time, however, the coureurs de bois system degenerated into a corrupt system that wielded great power and wealth, at the expense of the natural supply of beavers. Native Americans, who had long depended on beavers as a source of fur and food, quickly responded to the new demand for fur and in many parts of Canada, over-trapped the animals in a rush to acquire the new trading goods. Over time, the

142

Major trading routes were created around the beaver trade. When overland horse and wagon trails intersected water routes, settlements often developed, in some cases turning into cities, such as St. Louis, Missouri. This illustration is from the June 1859 issue of *Harper's New Monthly Magazine*. Illustration by W.A. Rogers.

value of beaver skins as a commodity also had a disastrous effect on some Indian tribes, influencing them to move away from their traditional territories, where they lived more or less in balance with natural supplies of food, to areas that had more beavers. This led to inter-tribal conflicts and wars, and some tribes eventually became malnourished or starved.

"For many years before the settlement of the country the fur of the beaver brought a high price, and therefore it was pursued with weariless ardor. Not even in the quest for gold has a more ruthless, desperate energy been developed. It was in those early beaver-days that the striking class of adventurers called 'free trappers' made their appearance. Bold, enterprising men, eager to make money, and inclined at the same time to relish the license of a savage life, would set forth with a few traps and a gun and a hunting knife, content at first to venture only a short distance up the beaver streams nearest to the settlements, and where the Indians were not likely to molest them. There they would set their traps, while the buffalo, antelope, deer, etc., furnished a royal supply of food. In a few months their pack animals would be laden with thousands of dollars' worth of fur."

— John Muir (1918, "Steep Trails")

At one point, some of the French traders chafed under new government trading restrictions that were ordered by French king Louis XIV, who attempted to maximize the profit to his country. These traders made secret deals with the English, then the enemy of the French, in order to keep more control for themselves. The English were ready and willing to grab a piece of the natural resources of Canada, and began sending trading ships into Hudson Bay to pick up cargoes of fur.

By 1670, the Hudson's Bay Company was founded as a monopoly, licensed by English king Charles II to handle all of the fur gathered in the watersheds feeding the bay. The success of the English traders soon escalated into heavy competition with the French, action that turned violent and involved military forces on land and sea. The battle that began over beavers dragged out for more than one hundred years, climaxing in full-scale warfare, with the English eventually gaining control of Canada from the French.

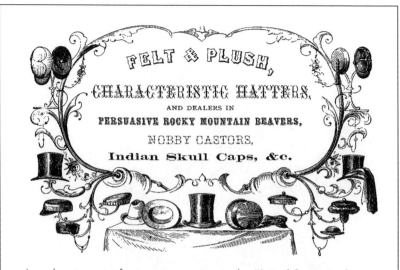

An advertisement from a newspaper in the United States in the mid-1800s.

Although beaver fur was long held in high esteem in Europe because of its rich, luxurious quality, it was beaver felt that triggered the greatest demand. Felt is animal hair that is pounded and pressed together to create a dense mat of material, used in making some articles of clothing. Felt making became a highly-developed craft in some parts of Europe, with high prices being paid for the best quality felt.

Felt was originally made from lamb's wool, until the underfur of some animals, including the beaver, was discovered to have the best natural qualities for making this material. About 1800, hat designers created a new style of top hat for men made from the finest beaver felt. These top hats, originally worn by nobility and the rich and privileged classes, quickly became a coveted and necessary part of the fashion scene from Moscow to London, as well as cities in the New World.

Beaver skins held a certain value depending on their size and quality. During much of the peak period for the beaver trade, these

As depicted in this illustration from the June 1859 issue of *Harper's New Monthly Magazine*, beaver pelts formed the basis of a widely-used standard of trade. Illustration by W.A. Rogers.

values were fairly consistant throughout North America. "Coat pelt" were those that had no guard hairs, consisting only of the downy undercoat. As this was the material most in demand for hats, coat pelts originally fetched the highest price because they required less processing. In their traditional use of beaver pelts for garments,

Native Americans made them into capes, worn with the hair to the inside. Over a season of wear, the guard hairs of these coat pelts gradually fell out from natural use.

"Parchment pelts" were freshly cured furs with the guard hairs still in place. For the first hundred years or so of the trade in beaver fur with Europe, parchment pelts fetched less money because they could only be processed in Russia, where specialized craftsmen had perfected a method — a trade secret — to remove the guard hairs. Eventually, when European manufacturers figured out how to do this for themselves, the price of parchment pelts increased and they were favored over coat pelts because they were usually fresher and had less damage.

At the height of the beaver trade, pelts sold in Europe for twenty times more money than they had been purchased for in North America. The underfur in one adult beaver pelt could produce enough felt to make about eighteen hats. Between 100,000 and 200,000 pelts were shipped to Europe each year from Canada alone.

Other designations for beaver pelts included "fat beaver," a plush pelt that had been sewn into a cape and worn; "demi-fat beaver," a plush pelt that had been sewn but not been worn; "muscovite beaver," a pelt that had neither been sewn nor worn; and "dry beaver," a pelt that had been dried or tanned but was in bad condition.

Beaver felt was used primarily in the making of hats and was widely used for this purpose for a few hundred years after the opening of trade with the New World. But around 1800, the most stylish gentlemen in London and Paris took to wearing top hats made from undyed beaver felt and triggered an outright fashion craze. Sometimes called "gray beavers" or just "beavers," the style swept through Europe and the Americas, creating an even hotter market for beaver pelts. But just as suddenly as this fashion trend appeared, it ended. It was the newly opened silk trade with China at the end of the 1830s that brought about this change. All of a sudden, fashionable men wanted only top hats made of silk and the bottom dropped out of the beaver market.

The peak of the trading era for beaver in the American territories was in the first few decades of the 1800s, while there was still a hot market for the pelts in the East and Europe; after that time, buffalo became a more valuable commodity. The volume and intensity of trading increased as major transportation routes were established, including the Oregon Trail and the Santa Fe Trail, as well as regular traffic on major rivers.

About 1821, the opening of the Santa Fe Trail and the growth of cities such as St. Louis on the Mississippi River prompted the first wave of white trappers to move into the western territories in search of riches from fur trapping. This movement was triggered by the actions of a few entrepreneurs, including William Henry Ashley, who set up businesses to recruit and equip men who were willing to undertake the long and dangerous treks necessary to find beaver in the western mountains. They advertised in local papers for adventurous men who might find such work appealing, helping launch the era of the mountain men.

In the Rocky Mountains, the mountain men generated a brisk trade in beaver pelts for about fifteen years. In 1825, they began meeting in annual get-togethers called a "rendezvous," the first held in Henry's Fork in what is now Wyoming. These meetings were used as a general excuse for entertainment but they were also important trading events, allowing fur buyers and sellers to exchange goods, money, and pelts.

Mountain men not only had to trap and skin the beavers, they had to keep themselves fed, insulated from the weather, and sometimes protected from hostile Indians. At the close of the winter season, when the prime trapping period ended, they also had to transport their bales of fur to the nearest trading posts or cities, sometimes involving distances of hundreds of miles. Using horses, mules, or canoes, a single trapper could carry 5,000 to 10,000 pounds of baled beaver fur. In 1825, a load of 9,000 pounds of beaver fur carried East by one mountain man earned him about $50,000, a fortune in those days.

The legendary mountain men of the Rocky Mountains earned their living trapping and selling beaver pelts. This illustration is by Frederic Remington, published in *The Century Magazine*, January 1889.

Mountain men were responsible for killing hundreds of thousands of beavers during the era when they were popular. In some areas, beavers were completely eradicated but in most regions, only the adult beavers were trapped, leaving younger ones to replenish the populations. Overall, the amount of beaver available to trappers began to diminish as the trapping culture spread, but it was fading demand rather than a lack of fur that eventually ended this period in western history. Beginning in the 1830s throughout the West, buffalo began to take over from beaver as the prime commodity just as supplies of beaver pelts began to diminish. In 1835, 50,000 buffalo robes were shipped out of Fort Union on the Missouri River, but only 25,000 beaver pelts.

The decline in beavers had forced some hat makers on the East Coast and in Europe to begin using other kinds of fur to make their felt. This included nutria and seal. But even as this shift was underway, the rapidly increasing sea trade with China introduced large quantities of silk, the commodity that soon mesmerized the fashion industry, leaving beaver in its wake. At the beginning of the 1830s, when the beaver trade was still booming, the price for beaver fur on the East Coast was $4 to $6 per pound. At the end of the 1830s, when silk had become the hottest material for hats, beaver fur was selling for $1 to $2 per pound.

In 1840, the last mountain man rendezvous was held in the Rocky Mountains. Although most of the native populations of beaver had disappeared, beavers were still found throughout most of the Rocky Mountains, the Sierras, and the Pacific Northwest.

HUNTING BEAVERS

"We are a busy people and we can give but little heed to sentiment, but surely there is time in our lives to think of preserving and protecting the beaver. Let us hope that the generations who follow us will be able to thank us, their forefathers, for having defended the beaver when they look on these small creatures continuing the work their Creator intended they should do."

— A. Radclyffe Dugmore (1914, *The Romance of the Beaver*)

Beavers have had triple bad luck. It's not just their luxurious fur that attracts attention from hunters, and the castoreum they secrete has long had a great value for its healing properties and use in perfume, but many cultures found beavers very good to eat.

In the Middle Ages in Europe, all three of these attributes were factors in the decimation of native beaver populations. At that time, beaver tail was considered more than just regular meat, it was a prime delicacy, fit for royal consumption. Some people considered beavers to be fish, not land animals, because they lived in the water. At one point, Catholics were allowed to consume beaver on Fridays — at least in Canada, where this kind of meat was available — when other types of meat were banned. This decision came in 1704, after the Académie des Sciences in Paris decided that the beaver's appropriate classification was with fish, not mammals, and this decision was supported by appropriate religious authorities in France.

Even though beaver meat did have a reputation as desirable for human consumption, in some parts of North America where these animals were abundant, the meat was fed to dogs instead. American Indians hunted beaver for fur and meat long before white trappers arrived. Beaver hunting was considered a great skill because the beavers were very wary animals and difficult to catch.

One favored method was to use deadfall traps placed along paths that the beavers used on their way to find fresh trees. A deadfall was made of a large log or group of logs, propped up with a stick in such a way that a beaver gnawing at the bait — usually succulent fresh shoots or twigs — would dislodge the prop and the falling weight of the logs would trap it or kill it outright. Beavers that were hunted for fur were in their prime in the fall and winter months and this was considered to be the best time for hunting them.

With ice covering a beaver pond, a hunter would use a knife or hatchet to make an opening near the lodge. Beavers often seek out such holes during the winter when the ice is solid as it provides them with access to fresh food and air. The hunter crouched near the hole and when a beaver popped up, knocked it over the head, much like Eskimos hunt seals through the ice.

Another approach was to attack the beaver lodge itself, even though these structures can be large and formidable. Several hunters with axes would break through the roof, causing the beavers to rush to their escape tunnels. But hunters using this method would first place woven nets or snares at each of the entrances, trapping the beavers as they escaped. Different styles of nets were favored, some made from plant fibers and others from animal sinew.

One special net design was created just for beavers. This design featured one or more openings just large enough for a beaver to stick its head through, thereby trapping it. In Labrador, native hunters would block the entrance to a burrow or lodge, then tear open the top and reach in to grab the trapped animals. Another ploy used by some subarctic tribes was to set rows of stakes in a beaver stream to create an underwater fence. An opening was left for the beavers to swim through, which was covered with a snare or a beaver net. Some hunters also favored tearing holes in beaver dams, certain to draw the attention of the resident animals. As they came to investigate the noise of water running through the broken dam, they would be speared or shot.

While careful planning, snares, and weapons were employed in the hunt for beavers, some Indians merely used their hands. In places where the terrain permitted, a hunter would lie patiently

To be effective, traps had to be placed in the water and baited with something to attract beavers, often a freshly cut branch from one of the beavers' favorite trees. This illustration is by A.B. Frost, for an article on beavers published in *Harper's Magazine*, January 1889.

next to a waterway until a beaver swam by, then grab it with his hands. The animals could also be shot with a bow and arrow. When hunting beavers, stalking was usually done at night, when moonlight provided appropriate illumination.

Beavers were hunted alone and by groups, and many Native American tribes trained dogs to help them in this activity. Beaver dogs were used in two basic ways. They could be attackers, crawling into burrows or lodges and forcing out the occupants for the human hunters to capture. Although it was possible for dogs to catch and

This illustration, by W.A. Rogers, is entitled "A Trapper Going His Rounds." Published in *Harper's New Monthly Magazine*, June 1859.

kill an adult beaver, the beavers were usually able to defend themselves, sometimes maiming or killing the attacking dogs. Hunters used the dogs instead to corner or chase the beavers into the open, where a kill could be made without damaging the valuable fur.

Other dogs were trained as sniffers, used to detect weak points in lodge roofs or burrows for their masters to dig. In the winter when beaver ponds were frozen over, these dogs were also capable of detecting where the beavers were hiding under the ice, allowing the hunters to break through and catch their quarry.

In northern regions where beaver were plentiful and found on most streams, native hunters might alternate streams from year to year, giving time for the beaver population to recover after it was targeted.

Beavers were often targeted as a source of meat, both in Europe and North America. Both the body and the tail provided desirable food, with the tail especially prized for its taste and as an important source of fat. In some North American Indian tribes, the feet were also considered delicacies. Mountain men and other settlers prepared beaver in a variety of ways, including roasted, fried, baked, and in stews. The tail might be roasted whole or cubed to boil in broth.

BEAVER CONTROL

"The house rose in conical splendor in the very center of the pond, the dam curving smoothly against the flow. Though it was not large, generations of beavers had worked there building this wilderness bridge across the creek."

— Sigurd F. Olson (1958, "Beaver Cutting")

Unhappily for beavers, when their populations expand and they extend their range, they often interfere with the activities of humans. Despite a general acceptance of them as desirable wildlife, their appetite for trees and other vegetation can cause alarm when carefully planted and nurtured specimens are targeted by the beavers for food. And their natural tendency to build dams can lead to localized flooding of lawns, pastures, fields, and roadways. In recent years, total damage from beaver activity in North America is estimated to be more than $100 million annually.

In one major multi-state survey, problems with beavers were classified mostly as flooding of roadways, fields, and pastures. Following this, they were also cited for the damage caused to commercial timber by flooding as well as damage and destruction of levees, dikes, and man-made dams. In the western states, irrigation canals and ditches are frequent targets of beaver activity.

In parts of North America where beaver populations first rebounded, these problems have been recognized for decades and appropriate measures have been developed to deal with them. Although not always successful, most communities and individual land owners can make adjustments that allow beavers to thrive without degrading the local quality of life.

At the extreme, live trapping is still practiced as an effective solution. Trapping may be practical not only as a way to remove an offending animal or animals, but because there are still regions and locations where beavers are desirable, providing relocation sites. However, if relocation areas are not carefully selected, the beavers

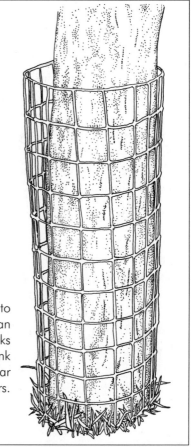

Most trees that are vulnerable to damage from nearby beavers can be protected by wrapping the trunks loosely with chicken wire, chain link fencing, hardware cloth, or similar kinds of metal barriers.

that are trapped and relocated can face unhealthy or fatal consequences, dumped where there is an unsuitable supply of food or too close to already-established beaver colonies. Stress, disease, competition, and bad timing can all lead to disastrous results.

Live trapping may only provide temporary relief. Even if troublesome beavers are trapped and removed from a location, the same natural forces that brought them there in the first place are likely to attract more beavers in the future. And with an expanding beaver population throughout most of North America, this becomes an even more pertinent factor.

If beavers are left in place, a variety of options can be employed to protect existing vegetation. The quickest, cheapest, and most practical solution is wire fencing wrapped around the trunks of vulnerable trees. When properly placed, these flexible barriers allow trees to grow while fending off the gnawing of the beavers. Typically, the fencing is wrapped around the base of a tree to a height of three feet or more, sufficient to thwart the reach of an adult beaver standing on its hind legs. In areas where winter snow depths can pile up and provide a natural bypass around these barriers, taller lengths of fencing are recommended. The bottom of this wrapping is staked to the ground with tent pegs, stakes, or other metal fasteners.

Fencing erected in its traditional form can also be effective in keeping beavers out of gardens, lawns, orchards, or other areas. As beavers are not very adept at climbing, relatively low fences are all that is needed to provide an effective barrier. In some locations, property owners have also made effective use of low-voltage electric fences such as those used for dogs or livestock.

Another deterrent, although not as effective as fencing, is the use of scent repellents. Beavers have an acute sense of smell and will usually avoid unpleasant odors, especially those that are designed to suggest the presence of predators. Fox urine, dog urine, coyote urine, and similar compounds sold as deer repellents can be used, but the downside is the strong odors that repel beavers will also prove offensive to humans. Although it is now widely banned because of environmental reasons, creosote has been a traditional compound used for beaver control; diluted and applied to tree trunks, it deters most beaver activity.

Beavers have a natural tendency to feed within easy reach of water. Their grazing forays into human neighborhoods will rarely be more than a few hundred feet from their regular watery base of operations. Therefore, greenery that is targeted for protection is usually limited to the extent of a local beaver's natural territory.

Beaver dams that create soggy conditions for humans create another provocation. But tearing down dams is not only difficult — beavers are capable of building large, formidable masses of tangled

As diligent as beavers are in their dam-building behavior, there are ways to overcome this activity. A variety of commercial devices are available for culverts and drains to reduce or eliminate blocking by beaver construction, and several methods can also be accomplished by hand. The most effective systems place a permanent drain well in front of the dam or inlet and apply simple techniques to keep these drains from being easily blocked by the branches or mud beavers use to repair leaks.

If the inlet side of a drain faces down into the water, the sound of the water entering a pipe is reduced, keeping beavers from being alerted to this telltale noise. Also, by pointing down, an inlet is virtually impossible to block up with mud or sticks.

Another effective design for the inlet side of drains relies on a perforated length of horizontal pipe extending at right angles from a dam or culvert. The number of inlet holes helps reduce the sound of draining water and the design is difficult to block up.

vegetation — it is often fruitless. Many cases have been reported of this kind of attempted fix with the local beavers ceaselessly active in rebuilding whatever damage has been inflicted by humans. Especially when dams are breached and not destroyed, beavers are often able to repair missing chunks in a single night. Nature has prepared beavers to be very persistent and persevering in their efforts; in most cases, the humans wear out before the beavers.

Typically, the small dams that most beavers build only cause problems when the beavers attempt to increase the water depth beyond a certain point. They are also attracted to certain kinds of running water, especially the sound of water rushing through openings such as culverts and drain pipes. This draws beavers to roadside sites where culverts are frequently used. In a short period of time, beavers can turn a functioning culvert into an effective dam, providing an appropriate body of water for their purposes, but not for the humans who put it there.

Engineers, entrepreneurs, property owners, and wildlife experts have all tackled this damming problem with a variety of effective solutions. Gates and barriers can be purchased to protect the inlet side of drainage pipes and a variety of commercial screens are made to thwart this kind of beaver activity.

All of these products follow simple basic principles. The main one is to provide a system of bars or screens that are not easily blocked by the vegetation or mud that beavers normally select to plug holes. Another factor is to reduce or eliminate the sound of rushing water that initiates the damming behavior in the first place. Some designs place intakes under the surface of the water or on the bottom. Inverted intake systems are also effective, drawing in water without telltale noise. At the outlet end, simply extending the length of a discharge pipe far from a dam site will keep the beavers from linking the sound to their own construction.

In much of their natural range, beavers are at home on larger lakes or deep rivers where they do not build lodges. In these habitats, their homes are burrows dug deep into banks, with the entrances underwater. This kind of burrowing activity creates additional problems for humans, because the banks that the beavers select for their homes can be levees, constructed to hold water inside specific channels. The large burrows that beavers build are capable of undermining levees, introducing erosion and breaks that have been responsible for flooding. Beaver burrows in sensitive locations such as levees can force live trapping and permanent relocation for the offending animals.

BEAVER RESTORATION

"The beaver is par excellence the builder among our native animals and the forethought evidenced by the dams and other structures compels interest."

— C.L. Herrick (1892, *Mammals of Minnesota*)

By about 1800, beavers were gone from most of their Canadian range, and by the 1830s, their population had been severely depleted in the Rocky Mountains. Even before this, local populations had long been gone from most of their natural range east of the Mississippi River. If any beavers were left, they were in small, isolated pockets and single colonies in remote areas. In New Jersey, the last beaver was gone by 1820; in New Hampshire, the same was true in 1865; Pennsylvania had none left by 1890; and the last beaver was trapped in Kansas in 1907.

At the time that Europeans first arrived in North America, the population of beavers was estimated to be from 40 to 80 million animals. By the end of the era of beaver fur trading in the mid-1800s, as few as 100,000 remained. Although the original populations had been decimated, scattered colonies of beavers remained in the Adirondack Mountains in New York, and in Maine, Michigan, Minnesota, Wisconsin, and Wyoming, as well as in Quebec, New Brunswick, and the other provinces of Canada.

Even before wildlife conservation became a public issue, people recognized the potential for permanent loss of beavers. Originally devised by fur-trading companies, plans were implemented in some areas of Canada by the mid-1800s to set firm rules and limits for the trapping of beavers so as to allow populations to recover and be self-sustaining. Beavers were also live-trapped and transported to new areas as early as the 1800s as part of these efforts.

At the same time, with hunting and trapping focused on other animals, beavers repopulated some areas on their own as the pressure from the fur trade diminished in the mid-1800s. Beavers

An illustration of beavers at work by A.B. Frost, from the June 1859, issue of *Harper's New Monthly Magazine*.

returned to stay in New Jersey in 1900, in Pennsylvania in 1901, in Virginia in 1915, and in West Virginia in 1922.

In less than a century, in fact, beavers in North America have rebounded strongly from being a species threatened by extinction to one that is thriving in most of its original range. Although less of a success so far in Europe, protection and reintroduction have increased beaver numbers there from a few thousand to several hundred thousand. Colonies of the North American species, *castor canadensis*, have also been brought to Europe to help speed up the recovery, but this effort may be hurting more than helping.

The North American species does not interbreed with the European species, *castor fiber*, even though they are extremely similar in anatomy and behavior. In places where the North American immigrants are thriving, they tend to out-compete the native species, threatening their survival. Possibly because of cultural differences, the North American beavers are also much more likely to build lodges and dams, improving their chances of survival in that climate compared to the natives. In any case, the current practice is to only use native European beavers in the effort to reestablish colonies.

Another beaver transplant effort that has gone awry is in South America. In Chile and Argentina, where beavers are not part of the native wildlife, breeding pairs were imported from Canada in 1946, an experiment intended to establish commercial fur production. In only a few decades, the lack of predators and the lush stands of local trees triggered a population explosion and gradual expansion in range. Beavers are now a major pest in parts of these countries, flooding farms and ranches and cutting down valuable timber. Wildlife experts in those countries now study the practices of beaver control professionals in Canada in order to help curtail the damage.

In parts of the United States, beavers are being actively live-trapped and transplanted to help extend their existing range. In places where existing beavers may be underpopulated, or the local population weakened by disease or flooding, transplanted beavers are introduced. In some urban areas, protected beaver populations wage a running battle with homeowners, park managers, and wildlife control officers. Although most municipalities now seem to support this kind of wildlife in urban settings, the animals can create havoc with ornamental plantings, carefully nurtured trees, and flood control culverts. Beavers that are too numerous can be thinned out and used to repopulate areas farther away from civilization.

One trend in some resort areas is a hearty welcome for beavers. Guests and residents in mountain areas find them to be an attraction, not a nuisance. A few resort developments have even begun to include beavers in the master plans for communities, with ponds and wetlands created by this natural force instead of bulldozers. Ranchers in some western states have also begun to rely on beavers to turn streams on their properties into ponds for a natural source of water for their livestock.

RESOURCES

Beaver Defenders
Unexpected Wildlife Refuge, Inc.
P.O. Box 765
Newfield, NJ 08344
609-697-3541

Beavers: Wetlands & Wildlife
146 Van Dyke Road
Dolgeville, NY 13329
beaversww.org

Canadian Wildlife Federation
2740 Queensview Drive
Ottawa, Ontario K2B 1A2 Canada
www.cwf-fcf.org

Canadian Wildlife Service
351 St. Joseph Blvd.
Hull, Quebec K1A 0H3 Canada
819-997-1095
www.cws-scf.ec.gc.ca

DCP Consulting Ltd.
Beaver Stop Division
3219 Coleman Road NW
Calgary, Alberta T2L 1G6 Canada
403-235-4620

Defenders of Wildlife
1101 14th Street NW, Suite 1400
Washington, DC 20005
202-682-9400
www.defenders.org

Forest Service/USDA
201 14th Street SW
Washington, DC 20024
202-205-1103
www.fs.fed.us

Friends of the Earth
1025 Vermont Ave. NW
Washington, DC 20005
202-783-7400
www.foe.org

Humane Society of the U.S.
2100 L Street NW
Washington, DC 20037
202-452-1100
www.hsus.org

**International Wildlife Education
& Conservation**
237 Hill Street
Santa Monica, CA 90405
310-392-6257
www.iwec.org

National Audubon Society
700 Broadway
New York, NY 10003
212-979-3000
www.audubon.org

National Park Service
1849 C Street NW
Washington, DC 20240
202-208-6843
www.nps.gov

National Wildlife Federation
8925 Leesburg Pike
Vienna, VA 22184
703-790-4000
www.nwf.org

National Wildlife Research Center
USDA Wildlife Services
4101 LaPorte Ave.
Fort Collins, CO 80521
970-266-6000
www.aphis.usda.gov/ws/nwrc

The Nature Conservancy
4245 North Fairfax Drive, Suite 100
Arlington, VA 22203
800-628-6860
www.tnc.org

Sierra Club
85 2nd Street, 2nd Floor
San Francisco, CA 94109
415-977-5500
www.sierraclub.org

U.S. Fish and Wildlife Service
1849 C Street NW
Washington, DC 20240
202-208-3100
www.fws.gov

The Wilderness Society
900 17th Street NW
Washington, DC 20006
202-833-2300
www.wilderness.org

Wildlife Services Program/USDA
4700 River Road
Riverdale, MD 20737-1236
301-734-3256
www.aphis.usda.gov/ws

The Wildlife Society
5410 Grosvenor Lane, Suite 200
Bethesda, MD 20814
301-897-9770
www.wildlife.org

Wildlife 2000
P.O. Box 6428
Denver, CO 80206
303-333-8294

World Wildlife Fund
1250 24th Street NW
Washington, DC 20037
202-293-4800
www.worldwildlife.org

World Wildlife Fund Canada
245 Eglinton Ave. East, Suite 410
Toronto, Ontario M4P 3J1 Canada
416-489-8800
www.wwfcanada.org

ONLINE RESOURCES

To find useful and interesting information about beavers on the World Wide Web, use a search program such as "google," "altavista," or "yahoo" with keywords such as "beaver" or "mammals." For a more targeted search, use additional keywords such as the common or scientific name of the beaver, "*Castor canadensis*." To find out about beavers in a general or specific geographic location, use the combined keywords of "beaver" and the name of the country, continent, state, or wilderness area. Also, try Web pages hosted by state wildlife departments, museums, wildlife preserves, zoos, and other animal organizations.

BIBLIOGRAPHY

Banfield, A.W.F. *The Mammals of Canada.* 1974, University of Toronto Press.

Benyus, Janine M. *The Secret Language and Remarkable Behavior of Animals.* 1998, Black Dog & Leventhal Publishers.

Bourlière, Francois. *The Natural History of Mammals.* 1954, Alfred A. Knopf.

Burt, William H., Grossenheider, Richard P. Peterson. *A Field Guide to the Mammals of North America North of Mexico, 3rd Edition.* 1980, Houghton Mifflin Company.

Chapman, Joseph A. and Feldhamer, George A., editors. *Wild Mammals of North America: Biology, Management, and Economics.* 1982, Johns Hopkins University Press.

Curtis, Edward S. *The North American Indian.* 1907, University Press. Republished in 1970 by the Johnson Reprint Corporation.

Dary, David A. *The Buffalo Book: The Full Saga of the American Animal.* 1989, University of Ohio Press. Originally published in 1974.

Dinsmore, James J. *A Country So Full of Game: The Story of Wildlife in Iowa.* 1994, University of Iowa Press.

Doutt, J. Kenneth, Heppenstall, Caroline A., Guilday, John E. *Mammals of Pennsylvania.* 1966, Pennsylvania Game Commission.

Fitzgerald, James P., Meaney, Carron A., Armstrong, David M. *Mammals of Colorado.* 1994, Denver Museum of Natural History and the University Press of Colorado.

Fleharty, Eugene D. *Wild Animals and Settlers on the Great Plains.* 1995, University of Oklahoma Press.

Freethy, Ron. *Man and Beast: The Natural and Unnatural History of British Mammals.* 1983, Blanford Press.

Frisch, Karl von. *Animal Architecture.* 1974, Harcourt Brace Jovanovich.

Gelder, Richard G. Van. *Mammals of the National Parks.* 1982, Johns Hopkins University Press.

Godin, Alfred J. *Wild Mammals of New England.* 1977, Johns Hopkins University Press.

Goodchild, Peter. *Survival Skills of the North American Indians, 2nd Edition.* 1999, Chicago Review Press.

Hadidian, John, Hodge, Guy R., Grandy, John W. *Wild Neighbors: The Humane Approach to Living with Wildlife.* 1997, The Humane Society of the United States.

Hafen, LeRoy R., editor. *Mountain Men and Fur Traders of the Far West.* 1982, University of Nebraska Press. First published in 1965 by the Arthur H. Clark Company.

Halfpenny, James. *A Field Guide to Mammal Tracking in Western America.* 1986, Johnson Books.

Hall, Edwin S., Jr. *The Eskimo Storyteller: Folktales from Noatak, Alaska.* 1998, University of Alaska Press. Originally published in 1975 by University of Tennessee Press.

Hall, E. Raymond. *The Mammals of Nevada.* 1946, University of Nevada Press.

Hall, E. Raymond. *The Mammals of North America, 2nd Edition.* 1981, John Wiley & Sons.

Hamilton, William J., Jr. *Mammals of the Eastern United States.* 1979, Cornell University Press.

Haney, Peter W. *Rodents: Their Lives and Habits.* 1975, Taplinger Publishing Company.

Hansell, Michael H. *Animal Architecture and Building Behaviour.* 1984, Longman.

Harding, A.R. *Fur Buyer's Guide.* 1942, A.R. Harding, Publisher.

Hilfiker, Earl L. *Beavers: Water, Wildlife and History.* 1991, Windswept Press.

Ingles, Lloyd G. *Mammals of the Pacific States.* 1965, Stanford University Press.

Jameson, E.W. Jr. *California Mammals.* 1988, University of California Press.

Landeen, Dan, and Pinkham, Allen. *Salmon and His People: Fish and Fishing in Nez Perce Culture.* 1999, Confluence Press.

Lowery, George H., Jr. *The Mammals of Louisiana and Its Adjacent Waters.* 1974, Louisiana State University Press.

Martin, Alexander C., Zim, Herbert S., Nelson, Arnold. *American Wildlife & Plants: A Guide to Wildlife Food Habits.* 1961, Dover Publications. First published in 1951 by McGraw-Hill.

Matthiessen, Peter. *Wildlife in America.* 1959, Viking Press.

McNamee, Gregory. *Gila: The Life and Death of an American River.* 1994, Orion Books/Crown Publishers.

Miller, Dorcas. *Stars of the First People: Native American Star Myths and Constellations.* 1997, Pruett Publishing Company.

Miller, Gerrit S. *Catalog of the Mammals of Western Europe in the Collection of the British Museum.* 1912, Trustees of the British Museum. Republished in 1966 by Johnson Reprint Corporation.

Mills, Enos A. *In Beaver World.* 1913, Houghton Mifflin.

Mills, Enos A. *Wild Life on the Rockies*. 1988, University of Nebraska Press. Originally published in 1909 by Houghton Mifflin Company.

Mitchell-Jones, A. J.; Amori, G.; Bogdanowicz, W.; Kryštufec, B.; Reijnders, P.J.H.; Spitzenberger, F.; Stubbe, M.; Thissen, J.B.M.; Vohralík, V.; and Zima, J. *The Atlas of European Mammals*. 1999, T & AD Poyser Ltd./Academic Press.

Murie, Olaus J. *A Field Guide to Animal Tracks, 2nd Edition*. 1974, Houghton Mifflin.

Murray, Andrew. *The Geological Distribution of Mammals*. 1860, Day & Son, Ltd. (London).

Nowak, Ronald M. *Walker's Mammals of the World, 6th Edition*. 1999, Johns Hopkins University Press.

Peterson, Randolph L. *The Mammals of Eastern Canada*. 1966, Oxford University Press.

Pielou, E.C. *Fresh Water*. 1998, University of Chicago Press.

Richards, Dorothy. *Beaversprite: My Years Building An Animal Sanctuary*. 1977, Chronicle Books.

Rue, Leonard Lee III. *Furbearing Animals of North America*. 1981, Crown Publishers.

Rue, Leonard Lee III. *The World of the Beaver*. 1964, J.B. Lippincott Company.

Ryden, Hope. *Lily Pond: Four Years With a Family of Beavers*. 1989, William Morrow & Company.

Sandoz, Mari. *The Beaver Men: Spearheads of Empire*. 1964, Hastings House, Publishers.

Schwartz, Charles W. and Schwartz, Elizabeth R. *The Wild Mammals of Missouri, Revised Edition*. 1981, University of Missouri Press.

Sterry, Paul. *Beavers and Other Rodents: A Portrait of the Animal World*. 1998, Todtri Productions Ltd.

The Trapper's Companion. 1946, A.R. Harding Publishing Company.

Tiner, Ralph W. *In Search of Swampland: A Wetland Sourcebook and Field Guide*. 1998, Rutgers University Press.

Walker, Deward E., Jr. *Blood of the Monster: The Nez Perce Coyote Cycle*. 1994, High Plains Publishing Company.

Warren, Edward Royal. *The Beaver: Its Work and Its Ways*. 1927, Williams & Wilkins Company.

Westcott, Frank. *The Beaver: Nature's Master Builder*. 1989, Hounslow Press.

Whitaker, John O., Jr. *National Audubon Society Field Guide to North American Mammals*. 1980, Alfred A. Knopf.

Wilsson, Lars. *My Beaver Colony*. 1968, Doubleday & Company.

INDEX

172

173

174

176

male beavers 28, 69, 72, 75, 76, 95, 128
mallard 134
mammals 47, 49, 52, 55, 59, 62, 74, 75, 127, 138, 140, 151
mammary glands 72
man-made dams 114, 156
man-made sites 22
maple 37, 82, 83
March 37, 72
marking territory 128
marshes 121, 138
marten 1, 16, 97, 98
mating 37, 72, 74, 76, 129
meanders 11, 115, 118
meat 1, 4, 5, 12, 23, 27, 151, 155
medicine 6, 15, 20, 23, 24, 27
medicine bags 24
medicine men 27
meetings 148
memory 20
Menominee 28
mergansers 134
messiness 83
metabolism 55, 68
Mexico 48, 53
mice 47, 50
Michigan 42, 97, 161
Micmac tribe 28
Middle Ages 20, 25, 151
Midwest 23
migration 37, 127, 129, 131, 132, 134, 136, 138, 140
military 25
milk 75
mink 10, 97
Minnesota 9, 161
misconceptions 2, 3
Mississippi Delta 53
Mississippi River 53, 126, 148, 161
Missouri 126, 148
Missouri River 42, 150
mistakes 103, 114, 121
mites 140
modern beaver 42, 43, 44, 45
molars 35, 62
molting 60
Mongolia 42, 54
Mongolian beaver 42
mongoose 25
monkeys 43
monogamy 37, 129

monster 19
Montana 22
moon 11, 16, 153
moonlight 153
morning 37
Moscow 145
moss 37, 84, 138
mother beavers 74, 75
motion 62
mountain beaver 38, 39, 50
mountain lion 97
mountain men 148, 149, 150, 155
mountains 22, 53, 164
mountain woodpecker 11
mouths 58, 122
mud 4, 35, 69, 94, 108, 109, 111, 112, 121, 124, 126, 128, 139, 159, 160
mud-hen 11
mules 148
municipal seal 7
Muridae family 47
muscles 47, 69
muscle spasms 23
muscovite beaver 147
musk bogs 128
muskrat 10, 12, 35, 38, 41, 102, 121, 127
myocastor 40
Myocastoridae 50
myths 2, 3, 8–19, 31–32

Narragansett tribe 28
Native American Languages 28
Native Americans 8, 13, 20, 28, 29, 142, 151, 155
natural protection 87
Navajo tribe 29
near-sightedness 62
nematodes 140
nesting chamber 109, 122, 126
nets 152
New Brunswick 161
Newfoundland 42, 53
New Hampshire 161
New Jersey 161, 162
New World 4, 7
New York 161
New York City 6
Nez Perce tribe 10, 11, 29
nictitating membrane 58, 62
night 153
nitrogen 139

177

180